THE Environment FIGHTS BACK

Ruth Naumann

NELSON
A Cengage Company

Australia • Brazil • Mexico • Singapore • United Kingdom • United States

The Environment Fights Back
1st Edition
Ruth Naumann

Cover designer: Cheryl Smith, Macarn Design
Text designer: Cheryl Smith, Macarn Design
Production controller: Siew Han Ong

Any URLs contained in this publication were checked for currency during the production process. Note, however, that the publisher cannot vouch for the ongoing currency of URLs.

Acknowledgements
Shutterstock: Images on the cover and pages 4, 7, 8, 9, 10, 11, 13, 14, 16, 17, 18, 19, 20, 21, 22, 23, 24, 25, 26, 27, 28, 29, 30, 31, 32, 34, 35, 36, 37, 38, 39, 40, 41, 42, 43, 46, 47, 48, 49, 50, 51, 52, 53, 54, 55, 56, 57, 58, 59, 60, 61, 63, 64, 65, 66, 67, 68, 69, 70, 71, 72, 73, 74, 75, 76, 78, 79, 80, 81, 82, 83, 84, 85, 86, 87, 88, 90, 91, 92, 93, 94, 95, 96, 97, 98, 99, 100, 101, 102, 103, 104, 105, 106, 107, 108, 109, 110, 111, 113, 114, 115, 117, 118, 119, 120.

U.S. Department of State (public domain): Page 5

Alexander Turnbull Library: Page 4, Hawkey, Allan Charles, Climate change?, 2 December 2010 (digital cartoons published in the *Waikato Times*), Ref: DCDL-0016254. Page 6, Moreu, Michael, And speaking of reducing waiting times ... What about the guy in the chair? He's been here ... 2008 (digital cartoons published in the Christchurch *Press* and Fairfax Media), Ref: DCDL-0008688. Page 5, Evans, Malcolm Paul, G20 Summit in Aussie. 14 November 2014, Ref: DCDL-0029933. Page 12, Evans, Malcolm Paul, 20 May 2008, Two frames, two cows, discussion about how to reduce carbon emissions, self-satisfied bull, Ref: DCDL-0006602. Page 24, Moreu, Michael, Attention visitors. 2 October 2014, Ref: DCDL-0030381. Page 28, Fletcher, David, 'Where do you want your billboard?' 'Cut down that tree and put it there.' 5 June 2002. *Dominion* (newspaper), Ref: DX-005-294, 'The Politician' cartoon strip. Page 43, Evans, Malcolm Paul, 2010. Robot with the letters of the word 'love' as part of its mechanism. Ref: DCDL-0016204. Page 53, Nisbet, Alastair, 'You want river access ... YOU GOT IT!', 17 June 2005, Ref: DCDL-0002621. Page 60, Moreu, Michael (digital cartoons published in the Christchurch *Press* and Fairfax Media), 'This report says dairying is a huge source of pollution. How are we going to tackle the problem? With scissors!', 12 February 2008, Ref: DCDL-0004974. Page 69, Darroch, Bob, 'Oh well ... at least it's filling up the hole in the ozone layer', 24 March 2014, Whangarei report (newspaper); *Timaru Herald* (newspaper), Ref: DCDL-0027765. Page 77, Binge drinkers, 14 May 2009, Smith, Ashley W. (digital cartoons published in the Shipping Gazette, MG Business, or Presto), Ref: DCDL-0011227. Page 78, Darroch, 'I don't know why they're complaining about NZ losing its GREEN image ...', 12 August 2013, *Timaru Herald* (newspaper); Whangarei report (newspaper), Ref: DCDL-0025827. Page 79, Ref: 1/2-046051-F. Page 83, Crimp, Daryl, DOC accidentally kill 800 rare snails, 11 November 2011, Ref: DCDL-0019443. Page 88, 'Rock snotting', Nisbet, Alastair, Date: 2005, published in *The Press*, Ref: DCDL-0005972. Page 89, Smith, Ashley W., Quarantine officials have been dealing with many biosecurity threatening packages mailed from overseas. 'Stand back folks!' 24 November 2004, published in New Zealand Shipping Gazette, Ref: DCDL-0004697. Page 97, Nisbet, Alastair, 'Okay guys ... are we prepared to enter fresh water? splutter!' 18 October 2012, *Press* (Christchurch, NZ), Ref: DCDL-0023240. Page 100, Nisbet, Alastair, Decontaminate, 10 August 2013, *The Press* (Christchurch, NZ), Ref: DCDL-0025910. Page 102, Nisbet, Alastair, Eastern recreational freedom camp out for Easter, 6 April 2015, *The Press* (Christchurch, NZ), Ref: DCDL-0031132. Page 105, Nisbet, Alastair, 'Clear off buddy! This is a toilet stop!', 1 December 2005, *The Press*, Ref: DCDL-0005964. Page 105, Hawkey, Allan, Surfing vision for the Waikato River – tourism recommendation, 2 February 2011, (digital cartoons published in the *Waikato Times*), Ref: DCDL-0016991. Page 110, Nisbet, Alastair, Verminrists, 12 March 2015, *The Press* (Christchurch, NZ), Ref: DCDL-0030783. Page 120, Hawkey, Allan Charles, 'The label reads "Best before WWII"', 20 April 2011, *Waikato Times*, Ref: DCDL-0017588.

For product information and technology assistance,
in Australia call **1300 790 853**;
in New Zealand call **0800 449 725**

For permission to use material from this text or product, please email **aust.permissions@cengage.com**

National Library of New Zealand Cataloguing-in-Publication Data
A catalogue record for this book is available from the National Library of New Zealand

978 017 041840 9

Cengage Learning Australia
Level 7, 80 Dorcas Street
South Melbourne, Victoria, Australia 3205

Cengage Learning New Zealand
Unit 4B Rosedale Office Park
331 Rosedale Road, Albany, North Shore 0632, NZ

For learning solutions, visit **cengage.co.nz**

Printed in China by China Translation & Printing Services.
1 2 3 4 5 6 7 21 20 19 18 17

Contents

World says *oui* to climate change deal in Paris

Climate change is when temperatures rise and oceans absorb much of the heat, which causes oceans to expand. Glaciers and ice sheets melt and sea levels rise. Most scientists say this is linked to human activities such as burning fossil fuels, for example oil and coal, which are non-renewable because they are made from decomposed plants and animals that have been buried in the ground for millions of years. Once used, they are gone.

Oceans absorb about a quarter of the carbon dioxide that humans produce each year. This makes oceans more acidic and is why many people call ocean acidification the evil twin of global warming. Ocean acidification threatens sea creatures by making it harder for them to grow shells. It also damages ecosystems by causing coral reefs to dissolve. Researchers are looking at ways to reduce this ocean acidification. For example, they have found that plants such as seagrasses and kelp can absorb carbon dioxide, and therefore planting them is helpful.

Some people say climate change is not happening. Most, like the man in the cartoon, believe it is happening and that human actions, such as industries emitting carbon dioxide, a greenhouse gas which can trap heat in the atmosphere and so make the Earth's surface warmer, are at least partly to blame. They want their governments to get involved in stopping it or slowing it down. Some experts say it might be too late to stop massive and bad results of climate change, such as extreme weather events, while other experts say it is not too late for the world to act.

ISBN: 9780170418409

New Zealand has a Minister for Climate Change Issues, and New Zealand is a member of the Intergovernmental Panel on Climate Change (IPCC).

IPCC

- is the international body for assessing climate change
- has thousands of scientists from all over the world contributing to it
- reports on the current knowledge about climate change to help governments make decisions about how to act.

In December 2015, a climate conference took place in Paris, France. Before and during the conference, countries made national climate action plans. At Paris, 195 countries — almost every country in the world — adopted the first-ever global climate deal, which experts said had a good chance of success. It was called the Paris Agreement. It said:

- Greenhouse gas emissions must peak (get to their highest level) as soon as possible.
- A global aim was to limit warming to below 2°C and to keep trying to limit it to 1.5°C.
- Developed countries (those with wealthy economies such as New Zealand) need to continue to take the lead in reducing emissions.
- Countries could decide for themselves how to lower their emissions.
- Governments would meet every five years to set more targets.
- Governments must report to each other and the public on how well they are doing in getting to their targets.
- Other groups such as cities, organisations and private business also had parts to play in addressing climate change.
- Rich countries would keep raising money to help poor countries transform their economies to cut down on emissions.
- A checking system was not to be a punishment but just to show when countries are off track so they can be helped to get back on track.

SKILLS PRACTICE

1 Key points (most important ideas)

List the key points about the Paris Agreement. Think of how global it was, emissions, temperatures, review, burden-sharing.

2 Linking graph to action

Before the Paris climate conference, Americans were asked, In your opinion, how important is it that the world reach an agreement this year in Paris to limit global warming?

In 2017, the US President said the US would stop taking part in the Paris Agreement. From your understanding of the graph, would you say everyone in the US agreed with the President's decision? Give your reasons.

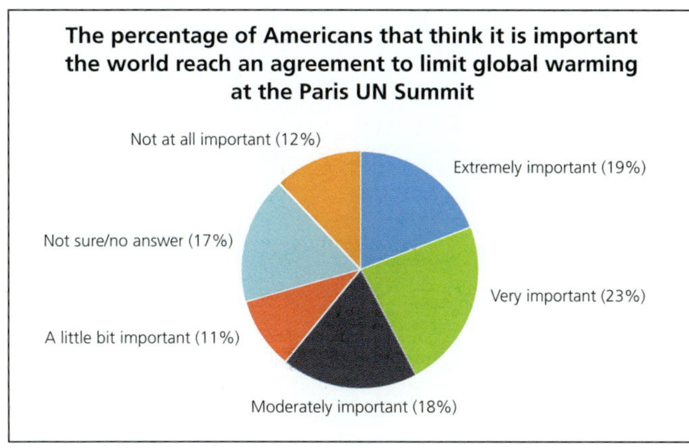

ISBN: 9780170418409

3 Cartoon themes (theme = subject)

Study the cartoons by Moreu (left) and Evans (right).

a Identify the common theme.

b Show how the cartoonists approach the theme in different ways.

c State why both cartoonists may have welcomed news of the Paris Agreement

4 Providing evidence (facts that show if something is true or not)

Find evidence for the following statements about the Paris Agreement.

a It marked a turning point in international climate talks.

b It showed an effort to get a low-emissions future.

c It encouraged NGOs (non-governmental organisations) to help reduce emissions.

d It departed from previous attempts at climate deals that had required all countries to adopt the same measures.

e It was to track progress towards the long-term goal through a friendly system.

5 Scenarios (possible developments)

Explain the three different scenarios the graph shows.

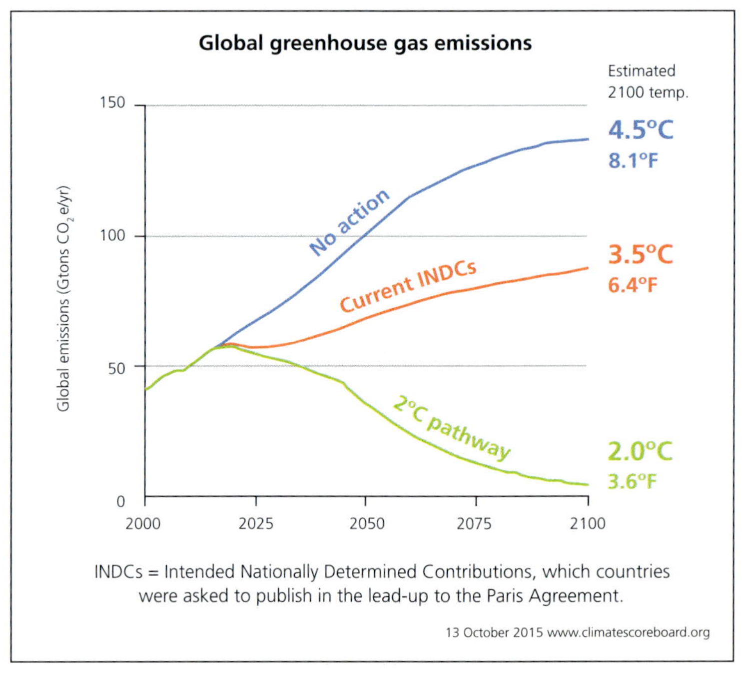

INDCs = Intended Nationally Determined Contributions, which countries were asked to publish in the lead-up to the Paris Agreement.

13 October 2015 www.climatescoreboard.org

ISBN: 9780170418409

Yanked away from Paris but US still into renewables

2

The US has been one of the biggest contributors to global climate change. When the newly elected US President said in June 2017 that he would stop taking part in the Paris Agreement, people wondered if it would weaken the global efforts to act on cutting out greenhouse emissions by using renewable energies such as solar and wind. Most experts said it wouldn't because renewables already had a good foothold in the US.

Researchers had a plan to get all 50 states on 100 percent renewable energy by 2050. Hawaii had committed to going 100 percent renewable by 2045. Washington, Iowa and South Dakota were on their way to a renewable future. Illinois and Michigan passed clean energy laws. California said it would work directly with other nations to fight climate change. In March of that year (2017), for the first time ever, wind and sun together made up more than 10 percent of US electricity. Experts predicted that by 2040 it would be 34 percent. The President, who was keen on coal energy and had expressed opinions, often by tweets, that climate change was fake news, had floated the idea of lining his proposed Mexican border wall with solar panels.

The US public was getting more interested in the goal of reaching 100 percent renewable energy by 2050. They got reports on how it could be done and how new technologies might go into the energy mix, such as military giant Lockheed Martin investing in wave and tidal energy. Solar energy was becoming a superstar. More people worked in solar than at oil rigs and in gas fields. In some states, new wind turbines generated electricity at a lower cost, without subsidies, than any other technology. Texas was the king of wind, and on some windy days supplied nearly half the state's power.

Many said the focus of the new president on fossil fuels was environmentally wrong because renewables were proving to be the energy sources making America great again.

People could feel they were part of a non-fossil future when the United Nations said that 2015 had represented a major shift in the global energy landscape when for the first time, the world added more energy from renewable sources than from fossil fuels.

SKILLS PRACTICE

1 Finding and using clues

Study the drawing and answer the questions about it.

a Who is the subject?

b What clues gave you the subject?

c What substance is the person drinking?

d What clues gave you the substance?

e How is the substance related to energy and what kind of energy is it?

f What clue suggests the subject is addicted?

g What clue shows the addiction is not good for the environment?

h Is it fair to say the subject represents everyone in the nation? Give a reason for your answer.

Addicted to oil.

2 Pinpointing (finding with accuracy)

Work out and copy out the sentence in the text that the graph best illustrates.

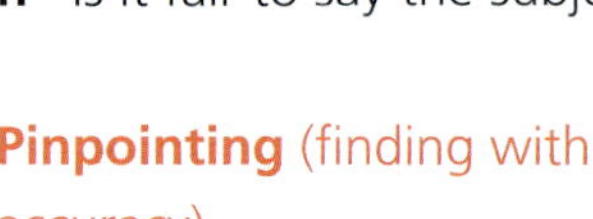

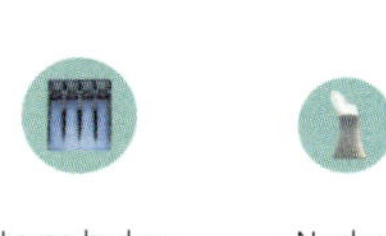

3 Graphs as evidence

Study the two graphs of capacities at this time and answer the questions.

a Why are the two energies known as renewables?

b How do they add to understanding of the US energy situation at the time?

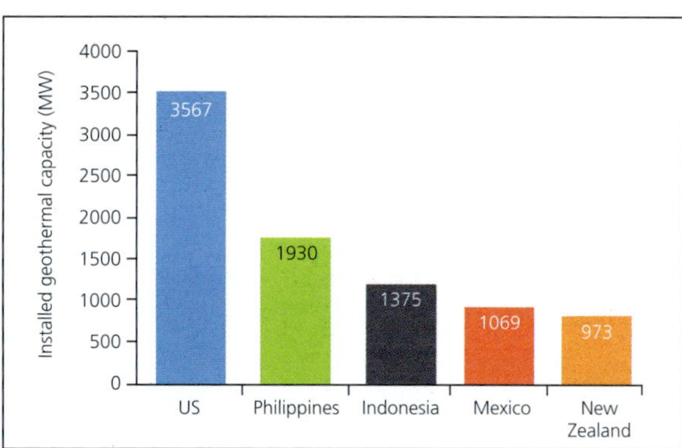

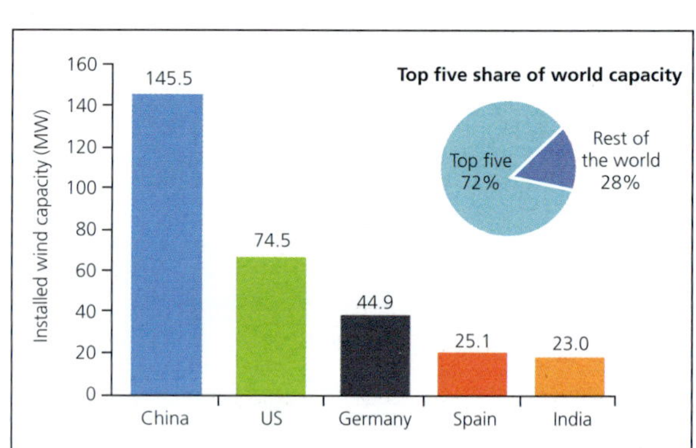

4 Philosophy (investigation of ideas about existence)

Make some notes about the following philosophical question that you can contribute to a discussion about it.

If a person invests in clean energy because its price is right and there is money to be made, is that person an environmentalist?

5 Thinking of the future

Prepare a diagram or piece of writing that shows your ideas of which route the US will choose for its future and why you think that.

ISBN: 9780170418409

China's choking catalyst

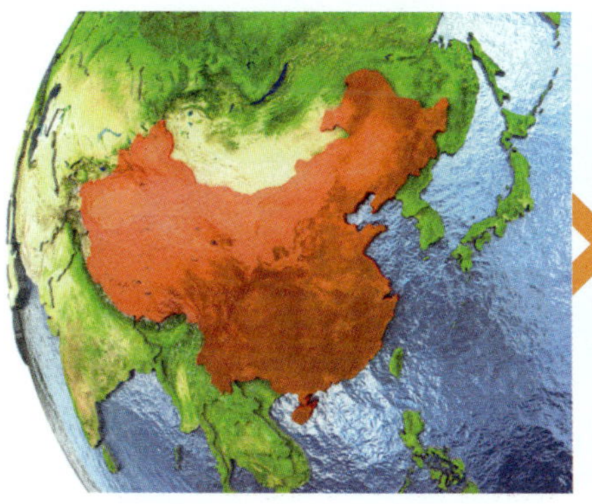

China is the fourth-largest country in the world and has the most people.

China's economy has become a superhero but now its billion-plus people need to turn into superheroes to fix the environmental problems the economy has helped to cause.

China is working to increase its protection and mending of the environment.

The Beijing smog of January 2013 = an environmental event with causes and effects

Smog is a mix of fog and smoke and other pollutants. The smog turned the city black, put people in hospital, and closed schools, airports and roads.

Causes

- Emissions from vehicles, coal-burning factories, families burning coal.
- Concentration of particles was 40 times the level that the World Health Organization said was safe.

Results

- An environmental turning point (catalyst), which showed people the harmful effects they are having on the environment.
- People complained and protested.
- Government acted by declaring war on pollution and a series of smog-busting measures such as making factories publicly report real-time figures on air emissions and water discharges, and cutting coal use.
- Government committed to moving away from fossil fuels to a low-carbon future.
- In a joint statement on climate change with the US, China committed to hit its peak carbon emissions by 2030 and to have renewables as 20 percent of its energy mix by 2030.
- Polls in China showed an increasing number of Chinese wanted the government to think of the environment first when planning economic growth.
- The Chinese Government announced that it planned to ban the production and sale of all diesel and petrol cars and vans. The future will be electric.

Providing people with nature reserves helps raise awareness of how special a country's natural environment is. This is Jiuzhaigou nature reserve. China has increased numbers of nature reserves and its massive volunteer tree-planting is expected to cover 400 million hectares, 42 percent of its land mass, by 2050. That would probably make it the biggest man-made carbon sponge in the world.

Recently, one of China's national symbols, the giant panda, was said to be no longer at risk of extinction, thanks to less poaching and more protection of its habitat (home environment).

SKILLS PRACTICE

1 Freehand drawing

Practise drawing freehand the shape of China.

2 Understanding catalyst

- **a** Name a catalyst for raising environmental awareness in China.
- **b** Describe the catalyst and its causes and effects.

3 Graph

Study the graph and answer the questions.

- **a** What monetary unit do the numbers represent?
- **b** Which location has the most new investment?
- **c** What pattern is there in the arrangement of areas?
- **d** What are ASOC and AMER?
- **e** In which area would New Zealand be?
- **f** Why does ASOC exclude China and India?
- **g** Why does AMER exclude US and Brazil?
- **h** In 2004, China invested $3 billion in renewable energy. How does that compare with 2015?

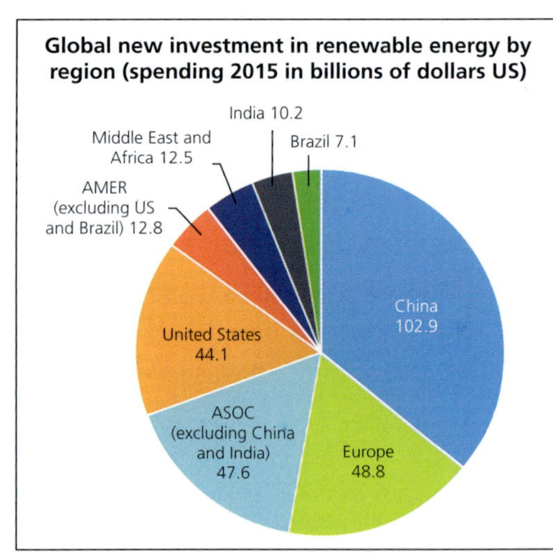

4 Being creative

Recently, China held its first painting competition for children on what we can we do to make Earth cool down, and 1.5 million children entered.

- **a** State what that signifies about environmental awareness.
- **b** Make an outline sketch for an artist to draw for a colouring-in competition for children on the theme of China helping its environment.

5 Thinking as an entrepreneur (taking on financial risk in setting up business, hoping to make a profit)

As a Chinese entrepreneur, think about which area you could look at for a business opportunity. Make some notes about your thoughts to share with others.

ISBN: 9780170418409

Stopping methane explosions from the paddock

4

- Methane is a greenhouse gas, which means it is bad for the environment.
- Cows, along with other animals such as sheep and goats, create methane through their digestive processes. The cows emit methane by burping or flatulence (farting).
- New Zealand's methane emissions from its animals account for a third of its contribution to climate change.
- Reducing this can help the government meet its emissions targets.

New Zealand is a leading researcher into ways to reduce methane emissions. Its projects include:

- a vaccine to reduce methane
- a slow-release chemical compound tablet to kill micro-organisms that produce methane in an animal's stomach
- breeding low-emission cattle and sheep to reduce methane emissions
- low-emission animal feeds and pasture crops.

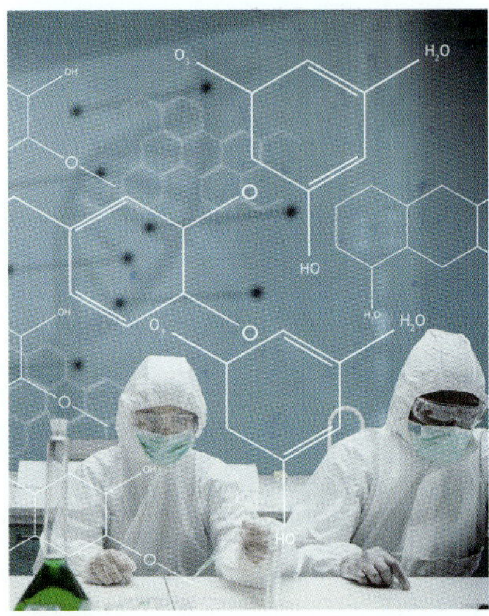

Other countries such as Australia, Canada, France and the USA are also researching ways to reduce methane emissions. For example, a Swiss company developed an inhibitor (a substance that slows down a process) that can reduce methane emissions by 30 percent per animal. It works only in a feed lot where the animal eats the inhibitor, but not in paddocks where animals can graze wherever they want.

The New Zealand Government is investing in providing leadership in the Global Research Alliance on Agricultural Greenhouse Gases — a voluntary agreement between governments to get countries working together in this research.

A recent study, largely funded by New Zealand in support of this alliance, examined more than 700 microbial samples from animals all over the world. The study found that methane-producing microbes were similar across different species. That meant if scientists developed a successful inhibitor in New Zealand, it could be adapted for use in other countries, and New Zealand would get recognition and economic benefit for developing a solution to help countries fight climate change by reducing greenhouse gas emissions.

SKILLS PRACTICE

1 Drawing a diagram

Sketch the outline of a cow, and use labels to show the following: what an emission is; where it emits methane from and where the emissions go; and why the animal is both good and bad for New Zealand.

2 Translating written data into visual

Methane emissions per animal/human per year: Western cattle 120 kg, non-Western cattle 60 kg, sheep 8 kg, pig 1.5 kg, human 0.12 kg (source: Nasa's Goddard Institute for Space Science). Make a visual to show relative sizes of emissions.

3 Cartoon analysis

Comment on the following.

- **a** The format (way it is constructed).
- **b** The actors.
- **c** The action.
- **d** Facial expressions.
- **e** Reference to carbon emissions.
- **f** Its effectiveness.

4 Elucidating (making something more lucid — clearer)

NZAGRC is the New Zealand Agricultural Gas Research Centre located in Palmerston North with a virtual centre of scientists located around the country researching for it. Its vision is to be an internationally renowned centre for research and development into agricultural greenhouse gas mitigation solutions.

State what 'mitigation' means here and give some examples of mitigation possibilities.

5 Values judgement

Microbes are the tiny bugs that keep the planet functioning and that could fit by the millions in the eye of a needle. New Zealand scientists are world leaders in microbes in the stomachs of cows and sheep that produce methane.

Do you think New Zealanders value the work of a scientist working in this field as much as it values the work of an All Black, and should it? Give reasons for your answer.

ISBN: 9780170418409

Germany's energy revolution

5

The algae house in Hamburg was the first algae-powered building in the world. It has an algae bioreactor front, which contains algae that are grown in sunlight, harvested, then turned into biofuel pulp that is burned in a generator in the building. Biofuel is produced from renewable sources such as plant and animal material. Algae are simple plants.

- Germany's energy supply is getting greener every year. Germany is in the middle of an energy revolution.
- By 2016, renewable energy was already 29.5 percent of energy generation.
- By 2025, 40–45 percent of energy consumed in Germany is to come from renewables.

The German Reichstag building in the capital, Berlin, home to the parliament, is a symbol of Germany's commitment to renewables. It produces more energy than it consumes through measures such as burning biofuel, and photovoltaic panels on its roof. Its famous dome has many energy-saving features such as a cone covered in 360 mirrors to reflect light into the parliament below.

(There has always been debate about whether nuclear energy is renewable or non-renewable. A common opinion is that because it uses uranium, which will run out one day, it is non-renewable.)

Action = 2010 and 2011, tens of thousands of Germans protested against Germany's nuclear energy.

Reaction = 29 May 2011, German Government announced it would close all its nuclear power plants by 2022.

ISBN: 9780170418409

Action = Renewable-energy subsidies in Germany have made solar and wind technologies more mainstream and cut their cost.

Reaction = Has helped other countries such as the USA, China and India install solar and wind power. Has busted the old idea that wind and solar are too erratic to rely on, because Germany, with all its wind and solar energy, is running one of the most reliable electricity grids in the world.

Action = German citizens given the legal right to be producers and suppliers of electricity to their grid system.

Reaction = The graph shows that as early as 2013, ordinary German people were part of the energy revolution through actions such as installing solar panels on the roofs of their houses and barns.

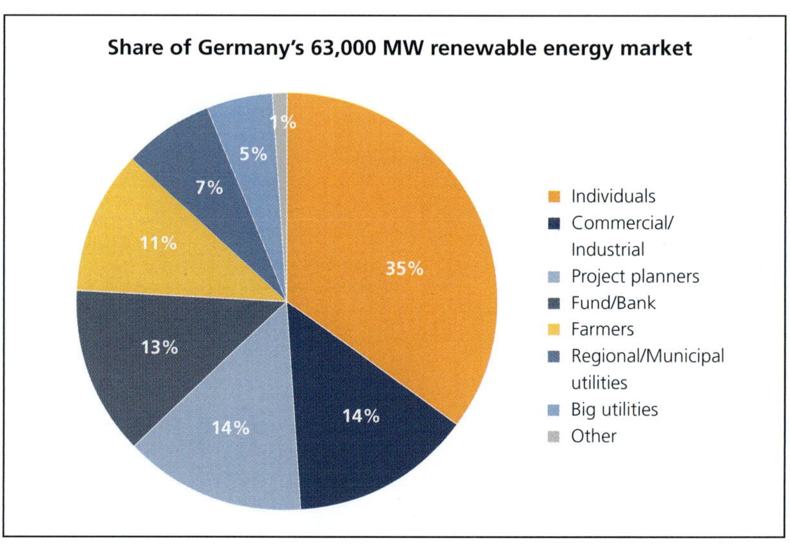

ISBN: 9780170418409

SKILLS PRACTICE

1 Referencing

State to what the following refer.

Hamburg's algae house; renewables; 360; 40–45; Reichstag; 2010 and 2011; 2022; uranium

2 Assessing difference

Refer to the graph below. State the difference between what Germany wants to achieve and what it had achieved when this graph was created.

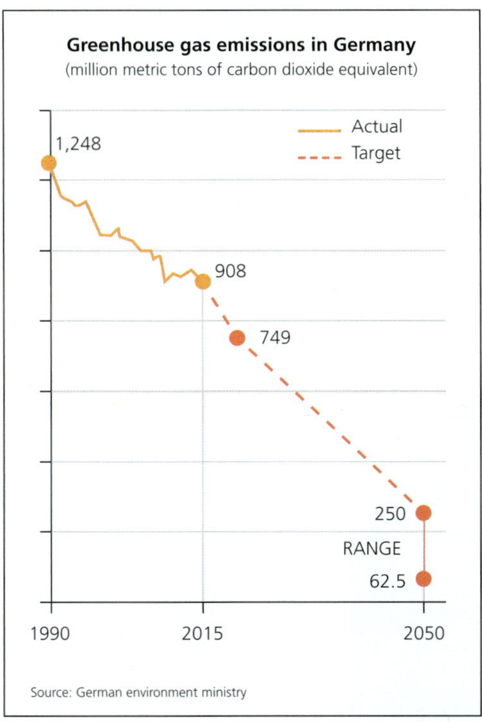

3 Understanding percentages

Refer to the graph on page 14 and answer the following.

- **a** What percentage did ordinary citizens have and how did you arrive at that percentage?
- **b** How does that compare to percentages for different professional groups?
- **c** What do the percentages show about giving German citizens an ownership and/or interest in the renewable energy market?

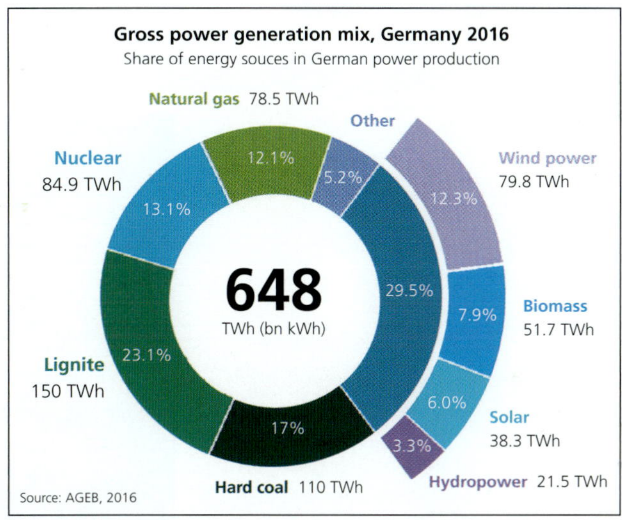

4 Understanding relating

- **a** How do the two parts of the graph (above right) relate to each other?
- **b** How is this relating shown?
- **c** What does the 29.5 percentage represent?
- **d** What is the biggest source of renewables?
- **e** Which percentage has already been mentioned in the text?
- **f** Which energy source is defined as organic matter used as fuel, especially in a power station for electricity generation?
- **g** Which energy source means a soft coal?
- **h** A terrawatt hour is a unit of electrical energy. What is its abbreviation and what is its relation to a kWh?
- **i** Into which category would oil fit?

5 Expanding

Germany has been called the world's first major renewable energy economy.

Expand the above statement into a paragraph by giving examples.

Anti-coal village in India goes into battle

- Coal has been the main energy source in India.
- Not only does coal produce greenhouse gas emissions when it burns, it also causes pollution when it is mined and when it is transported from its source.
- In the early 2000s, the government began a programme to bring coal energy to hundreds of millions of Indians.

The state of Andhra Pradesh was to get seven large and 30 smaller coal-powered power stations. In 2008, one such large power station was to be built at a town called Sompeta on land that included wetland. This wetland lessened the effects of natural disasters such as tidal waves, provided breeding grounds for birds, and a living for farmers and fishermen.

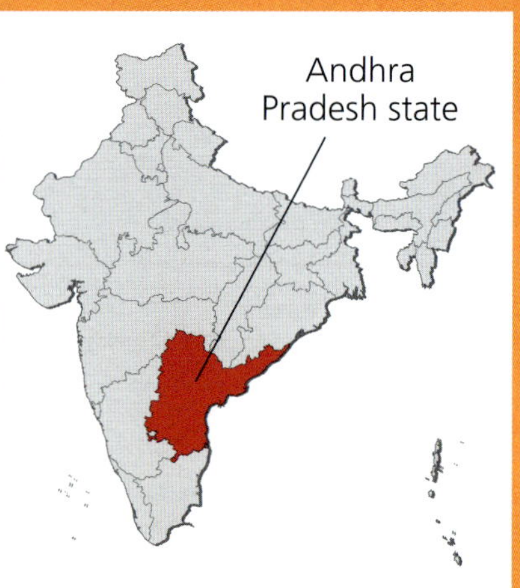

People of the community did not want the power station. They went on relay hunger strikes. They wrote letters of protest, held meetings, made public speeches, sent petitions, held street marches. They demonstrated at the construction site and when police used batons against them they threw stones. Two people were killed and many were injured.

In 2011, a judge suspended the government order allocating land to the power plant. In 2015, the state government cancelled the land allocation for the power station and said the company could use the land only for projects that were environmentally friendly. Later, with banks offering loans and the state government offering subsidies, locals began using solar energy.

At that time, 70 percent of India's power came from coal, and a study showed India would not be able to meet its Paris climate agreement commitments if it built the coal-fired power plants.

ISBN: 9780170418409

India announced a goal to increase solar power capacity to 100 gigawatts (GW) by 2022. At that time the world's total installed solar power capacity was 181 GW. But investors from all over the world were showing an interest in India's growing solar sector.

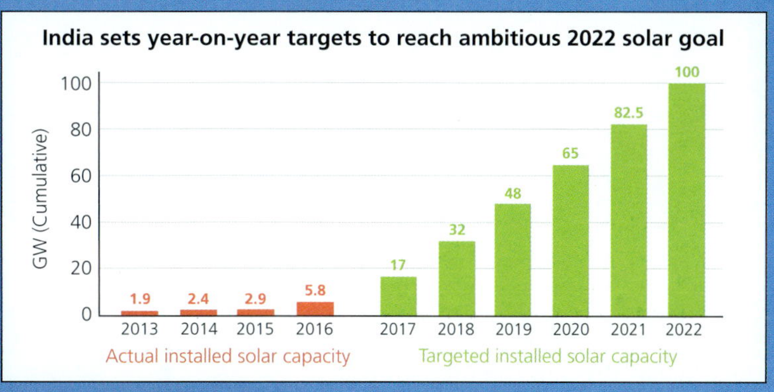

SKILLS PRACTICE

1 Emotional language (designed to get reaction)

Read the report below and rewrite it to remove all the emotion.

In July 2010, more than 3000 fearless community members at Sompeta engaged in an inspiring David versus Goliath struggle as they fought plans to sacrifice their land, their water, their air and their livelihoods for a coal plant, the decision of their unthinking government. Their protest got a brutal response, including the murder of three of their brothers. This brave struggle galvanised public opinion and buried the project where the coal should have stayed — in the ground.

2 Multi-choice

Write out the sentences using the correct alternatives for each.

- **a** India's 2022 target was (low, medium, high).
- **b** The 2022 target was for (fossil fuel, renewable energy, non-renewables).
- **c** The state of Andhra Pradesh is (landlocked, on the coast, in the north).
- **d** World entrepreneurs were (interested in, uninterested in, critical of) India's growing solar energy.
- **e** As far as the Paris Agreement was concerned, by 2017 India (planned to meet its commitments, had pulled out of it, had given up aiming for cleaner energy).

3 Getting meaning from a graph

Refer to the graph above of India's solar goal and answer the questions.

- **a** What year was the graph prepared and how do you know that?
- **b** What measurement is used for solar power?
- **c** What measurement is on the y-axis?
- **d** What data is on the x-axis?
- **e** What sort of graph is it?
- **f** What is meant by the terms 'actual' and 'targeted'?
- **g** What does 'capacity' mean?
- **h** For how many years was the goal set?
- **i** At this time, the cost of solar power was in freefall. How might that impact on India reaching its goal?

4 Identifying

Identify the main players in the Sompeta story from beginning to end.

5 Looking at conflict

- **a** State the methods used during the conflict.
- **b** State how the conflict was resolved (sorted out).

Shining lights for low-carbon future

A low-carbon economy =

- specifically refers to the greenhouse gas carbon dioxide
- generally refers to little output of greenhouse gas emissions
- low-carbon power sources
- a shift away from fossil fuels.

After the Paris Agreement, the world was more alert to shining lights for a low-carbon future, including the following examples.

For its 2016 climate talks often known by the abbreviation COP22 (22nd Conference Of the Parties), the United Nations hosted global leaders in Marrakesh in Morocco. Morocco was a good role model for getting other countries behind the Paris Agreement. It had stopped fossil fuel subsidies and was building the world's largest solar plant.

The world got its first solar highway — a stretch of road nicknamed the Wattway and paved with solar panels giving enough energy to power the street lights of the small French town of Tourouvre-au-Perche. In theory, said experts, France could become energy independent by paving only a quarter of its one million kilometres of road with solar panels.

Industry giants such as Walmart, Google, Apple and Mars committed to power their operations with 100 percent renewable energy.

For the first time, spending on clean energy in emerging countries in South America, Africa, the Middle East and Africa outdid that in richer countries.

Investment in the low-carbon future was growing. For example, Deutsche Bank was to provide billions of dollars for clean energy in sub-Saharan Africa.

A group of businesses offered to help the UK Government come up with a new plan to fight climate change. The group wanted an energy-efficient drive such as decarbonising buildings.

ISBN: 9780170418409

Pay-as-you-go off-grid solar companies arrived in Africa. For example, with a $30 deposit and daily 50-cent payments, all by mobile phone, a customer got a solar panel, lights, a phone charger and a solar-powered radio. Basic systems had enough grunt to charge phones and lights, and larger systems could power small items like radios and televisions. After the first year of payments, the customer owned the system.

About 150 groups had worked together to develop Low Carbon Auckland and the plan was to act on it so Auckland could join the list of the most environmentally friendly cities of the world, all of which had an active approach to fighting climate change. Examples were Amsterdam (more bikes than people), Copenhagen (windmills), Oslo (public transport), Freiburg (car-free suburb).

SKILLS PRACTICE

1 Knowing your terms

Write definitions for the following.

fossil fuels; the Wattway; sub-Saharan Africa; decarbonising; Mars; subsidies; Walmart; energy-efficient; Deutsche Bank; off-grid

2 Recalling

Study the image for *one* minute, turn the book over so you can't see it, then try to reproduce it. You could label it to show colours and features.

New energy for the planet.

ISBN: 9780170418409

3 Matching

Write out the following statements and beside them, state which items in the text they best match.

- **a** Sceptics are waiting to see whether the panels can cope with time, weather, and the beat-up from trucks.
- **b** The average Tanzanian will consume as much power in eight years as an American consumes in one month.
- **c** They said that taking such measures would be good for the British economy and the environment.
- **d** The previous year, this city had been voted the most popular tourist destination on the planet and now it was hosting one of the most important — if not the most important — international conferences ever.
- **e** It replaces kerosene fuel and gas-powered generators that pollute the air and are fire hazards.
- **f** Today, cities around the world are at the forefront of a global transformation to a sustainable low-carbon future.

4 Considering change

Explain how this graph would have to change by 2030 if the UK was more low-carbon.

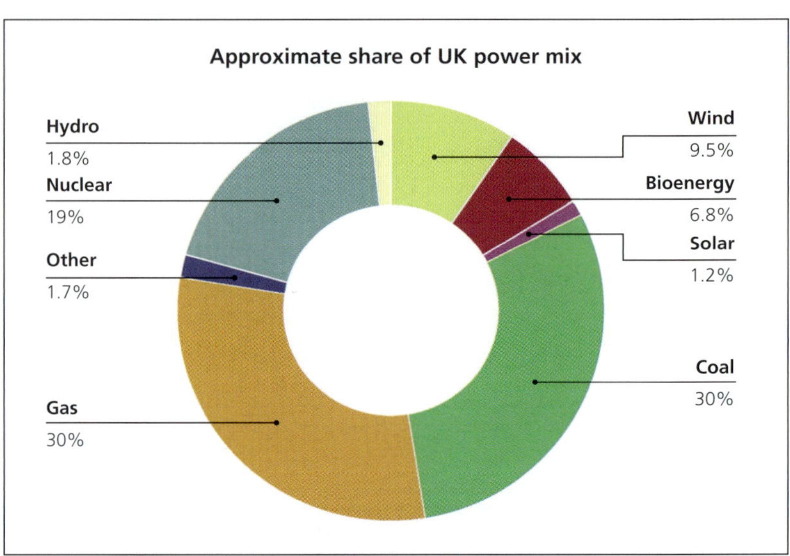

5 Linking

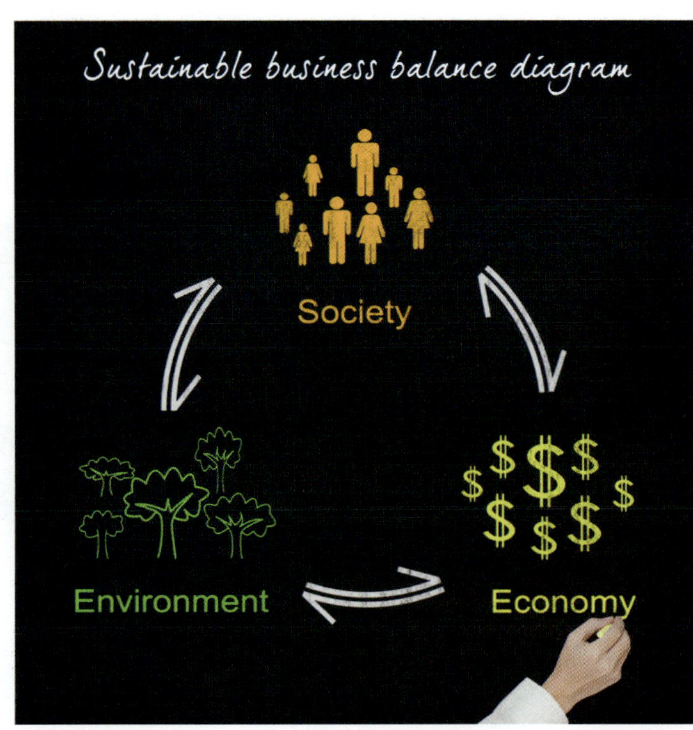

'We offer our support and expertise as a group of organisations that can play a crucial role in delivering the emissions cuts the UK needs to achieve, in addition to creating jobs and boosting economic productivity.'

(Extract from a letter that businesses sent to the UK Government to offer help to become low-carbon.)

Make a copy of the image and use the extract to add material to it to show the links more fully.

ISBN: 9780170418409

Earth Summits shove the environment to the top

8

A summit is the top, and a summit meeting is a meeting of top people, usually heads of government.

The Earth Summit = the World Summit on Sustainable Development (making sure resources such as water are available for future generations), a United Nations global conference to find ways to look after Earth's environment.

1972 First Earth Summit, held in Stockholm, Sweden. For the first time, governments put environmental issues on the international agenda, and said that human action had damaged the environment and that they had to work together on issues such as getting alternative sources of energy to replace fossil fuels, which they linked to global climate change. It produced the Declaration of the United Nations Conference on the Human Environment, which said natural resources must be protected for present and future generations, and it produced the UNEP (United Nations Environment Programme) to encourage helping the environment around the world.

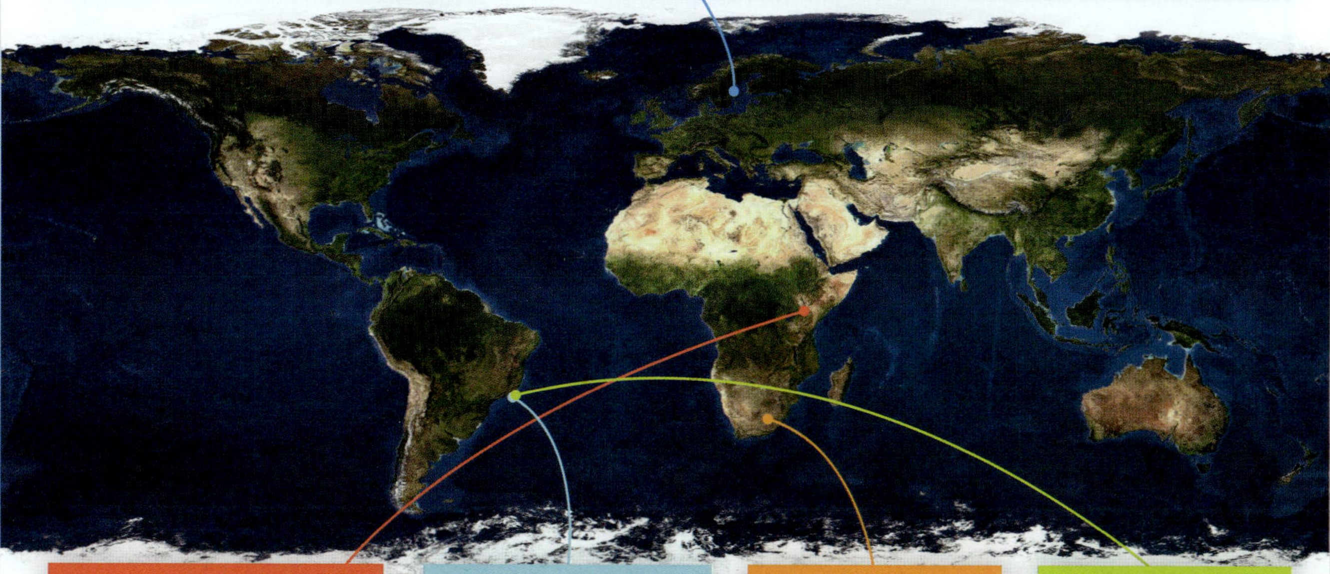

1982 Earth Summit in Nairobi, Kenya. Issues such as climate change were starting to move from something only scientists knew and talked about to something that ordinary people could learn about.

1992 Earth Summit in Rio, Brazil. Global warming was the major issue, and a protocol (official document) asked signatories to cut carbon dioxide emissions.

2002 Johannesburg, South Africa. It said water and sanitation, energy, health, agriculture and biodiversity needed special attention.

2012 Rio, Brazil. It adopted conventions (agreements among countries) on biological diversity, fighting desertification, and climate change.

Other international conferences, such as the 2016 United Nations Climate Change Conference in Morocco, are linked to Earth Summits because they deal with the same issues such as reducing greenhouse gas emissions, and limiting global temperature increases.

SKILLS PRACTICE

1 Matching

State which images match the locations of the Earth Summits on page 21.

2 Understanding logistics (detailed organisation of complex operations)

List things that organisers of Earth Summits have to think about, such as security, and finding a suitable building. For example, the 2012 Summit was billed as the biggest UN event of all time, with 15,000 soldiers and police guarding delegates from 192 countries and the 45,000-plus individuals gathered in Rio for the 10-day mega-conference.

3 Speech-making

Seventeen-year-old New Zealander Brittany Trilford was invited to give the opening speech at the 2012 Earth Summit. She told her listeners that they had promised to look after the environment by measures such as fighting climate change and pollution and yet the environment was still in danger and time was running out. Do something, she said.

Imagine you have been invited to present the opening speech to the next Earth Summit. Prepare your introductory paragraph.

4 Multi-choice questions

Answer the following.

- **a** The Earth Summits are held every: A two years, B five years, C 10 years.
- **b** The message to keep the oil in the soil and the coal in the hole relates best to: A fossil fuels, B biodiversity, C desertification.
- **c** The Earth Summit referred to as Rio+20 would have been in: A 1992, B 2002, C 2012.
- **d** The United Nations is to the Environment Programme as the Earth Summit is to: A Climate System, B Sustainable Development, C Human Environment.
- **e** The word 'signatories' is most sensibly paired with: A speech, B protocol, C scientists.

5 Assessing delivery

Say this image represents different stages in international efforts to make sure Earth Summits deliver global sustainable development. State which stage best represents where Earth Summits are at present and why you think this.

ISBN: 9780170418409

Earth gets a charter

In 2000, world leaders gave Earth a charter (a formal document that includes rights). It wanted to get people to understand how the health of the environment is essential to human wellbeing and how every human should share in the responsibility of preserving the environment for future generations.

Excuse me, but do I go to your local market and steal all the snacks?

Why create an Earth Charter? The Earth Summits had encouraged people around the world to get involved in protecting the environment. The United Nations wanted a charter to guide people towards getting a sustainable future (a future where all the resources hadn't been used up).

How was the Earth Charter created? It took six years to write, with people around the world consulted and thousands of organisations supporting it.

Where was it launched? It was launched in 2000 at a ceremony at the Peace Palace in The Hague. At the 2002 Earth Summit, a copy of it was put in a wooden chest called an Ark of Hope.

The Peace Palace in the Dutch city of The Hague.

How was it received? Today, an increasing number of international lawyers recognise that the Earth Charter is getting the status of a soft law document. Soft law documents are considered to be morally, but not legally, binding on governments that agree to adopt them, and they often form the basis for the development of hard law (laws that are legally binding).

How long is it? Compared to most United Nations documents, it is very short, only four pages long.

What does it say?

- Earth provides an environment necessary for humans to live such as variety of plants and animals, fertile soils, pure waters, and clean air.
- Every human has a responsibility to care for the environment.
- Humans have to decide to either form a global partnership to care for Earth or risk the destruction of it.
- Humans need to change their thinking.
- Humans need to learn that when basic needs have been met, human development is mainly about being more, not having more.
- Humans have the knowledge and technology to reduce their impacts on the environment.
- Humans should examine their values and choose a better way.

SKILLS PRACTICE

1 Paraphrasing (putting into different words to get better understanding)

Paraphrase the following points from the Earth Charter.

- **a** Respect and care for the community of life.
- **b** Respect Earth and life in all its diversity.
- **c** Care for the community of life with understanding, compassion and love.
- **d** Secure Earth's bounty and beauty for present and future generations.
- **e** Protect and restore the integrity of Earth's ecological systems, with special concern for biological diversity and the natural processes that sustain life.
- **f** Prevent harm as the best method of environmental protection and, when knowledge is limited, apply a precautionary approach.
- **g** Adopt patterns of production, consumption and reproduction that safeguard Earth's regenerative capacities.
- **h** Advance the study of ecological sustainability and promote the open exchange and wide application of the knowledge acquired.

2 Assessing a response

The Earth Charter was a response to a challenge. State what you think the cartoonist who drew this cartoon in 2014 may have thought of New Zealand's response to the Earth Charter. State reasons for your verdict.

ISBN: 9780170418409

3 Understanding cause and effect

Create a diagram to show how the creation of the Earth Charter was an event that had cause/s and effect/s.

4 Being positive

List as many positive things about and to do with the Earth Charter as you can.

5 Ordering

Put the images in order of most emotional illustration of the Earth Charter to the least emotional. Justify your order.

What if they screamed?

Some ancient societies worshipped trees. Those societies would be upset to see how much forest cover has gone from Earth today. They would, however, be pleased to see how many societies are again appreciating just how much trees do for the environment and why humans are starting to make sure they don't give trees cause to scream.

The good things that trees do

- Provide habitats and food for birds and other animals.
- Absorb carbon dioxide from the air and store it.
- Release oxygen.
- Help prevent soil erosion.
- Reduce runoff by breaking rainfall.

Felix Finkbeiner of Germany was 13 years old in 2011 when he delivered a speech to the United Nations in New York about climate change. He said, 'We children know adults know the challenges and they know the solutions. We don't know why there is so little action.' As a nine-year-old, Felix had done a school assignment on climate change and put into it the idea that the children of the world could plant a million trees in every country. By the time of his speech, Germany had planted its millionth tree and Plant-for-the-Planet, the environmental group Felix founded to raise awareness among children and adults about climate change, had been officially launched and had an army of 55,000 young climate ambassadors. By 2017, Plant-for-the-Planet, along with the United Nations Billion Tree Campaign, had planted more than 14 billion trees in more than 130 countries and was aiming to plant one trillion trees — 150 for every person on the planet. Those trees could absorb a massive amount of carbon dioxide, which Felix said would buy time for the world to get serious about reducing carbon emissions.

ISBN: 9780170418409

The New Zealand Trees That Count project aims to get Kiwis to plant millions of native trees to fight climate change, and to help the environment.

Millions = one tree planted for every New Zealander = e.g. on 6 October 2017 that was 4,717,399.

Native trees = trees that always grew in New Zealand such as kauri, pohutukawa, northern rata, kowhai, matai, kawaka, red beech, black beech, titoki, rewarewa, manuka, rangiora, totara, rimu, kahikatea.

That count = keeping a live count of the number of native trees being planted + planting trees that count for climate change + recognising the work that thousands of Kiwis do each year + measuring the impact on climate change.

Funded = Tindall Foundation (family trust of the man who created The Warehouse company).

Partners = Project Crimson Trust (organisation to plant and protect pohutukawa and its cousin rata), DOC (Department of Conservation to protect and restore species, places and heritage), Pure Advantage (group which wants a greener future for New Zealand).

A few hours after the signing of the Paris Agreement on climate change in New York in April 2016, busloads of volunteers from Christchurch's Student Volunteer Army went to the Tuhaitara Coastal Park to plant 2000 native trees as the first step in a five-year programme to set up a forest in the park. This action was a response to the Paris Agreement calling for communities, as well as governments, to take action on climate change. The trees were the first 2000 in the ground funded by Trees That Count.

SKILLS PRACTICE

1 Understanding a cycle

State the role of the tree in the carbon cycle.

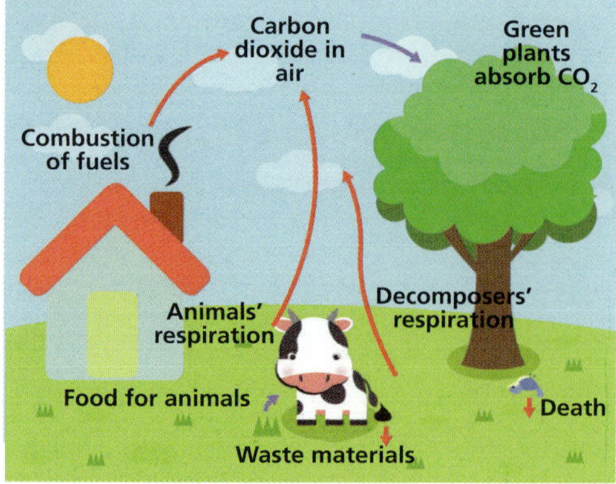

2 Assessing actions

a Refer to the two images and state which human action is best for the planet and why.

b List the native trees mentioned on page 27 and learn their spellings.

3 Demonstrating how

The world is always being told to plant trees but many people don't know how to plant a tree.

Using a labelled sketch or text or any other means, demonstrate how to plant a tree. Include where to plant it. For example, a pohutukawa planted in a tiny garden right beside the wall of a house will soon cause problems.

4 Finding features

List features that Plant-for-the-Planet and Trees That Count have in common and things they don't have in common.

5 Assessing sincerity (honesty)

State how the cartoonist has raised the question of the MP's sincerity.

 ISBN: 9780170418409

World should samba for Brazil

Amazonia is the largest tropical forest in the world, being about five million square kilometres.

Brazil contains about 60 percent of the entire Amazon forest. It is the largest tropical forest country in the world. At the peak of its deforestation (getting rid of trees) in 2004, it was the world leader in deforestation.

Deforestation is bad news for the environment. It puts larger amounts of greenhouse gases into the atmosphere. With no forest to soak up rain gradually, more floods and droughts occur. It takes habitats from animals and plants. It can be a never-ending cycle because as soon as the deforested area becomes no longer fit for purpose, farmers and cattle ranchers, and loggers and miners, get rid of more forest.

But now some good news.
Brazil has been *decreasing* deforestation.

ISBN: 9780170418409

How it happened

Groups working to save rainforest joined up to create the Zero Deforestation campaign to put pressure on the government.

A Greenpeace report linked the soybean industry to deforestation, global warming, and water pollution. It focused on Cargill (giant grain trader and exporter) and McDonald's (world's largest fast food chain).

Cargill and McDonald's said no more buying soybeans produced on Amazon farmland deforested after a specific date. Later, the same action was taken for beef.

The Brazilian Space Agency used its DETER satellite to monitor changes in forest cover in real time, and showed deforestation hotspots for law enforcers to chase up illegal loggers.

Brazil's new government began to change people's attitudes by saying rainforests belonged to all Brazilians and destroying it wasted precious resources.

Government got tough on rainforest crime. It patrolled roads leading into rainforest, gave out high-profile fines for people illegally damaging rainforest, seized illegal timber, closed illegal sawmills, and jailed people, including government officials who had been taking bribes to look the other way.

Government set aside over half of the Brazilian Amazon for national parks or indigenous (native Indian) lands.

The United Nations set up the Reducing Emissions from Deforestation and Forest Degradation in Developing Countries (REDD+) programme. Industrialised countries with high carbon emissions pay for carbon storage by preserving forests in developing countries. Norway, for example, pledged a billion dollars to rainforest preservation in the Amazon. Brazil was paid only after measurable decreases in deforestation had been seen.

Results

- Brazil cut greenhouse gas emissions more than any other country.
- It showed that reducing deforestation could be done quickly.
- It was a role model for countries of high deforestation such as Indonesia.
- Research institutes showed people how they could increase productivity without deforestation.
- Brazil's cattle herd and soybean production continued to increase despite the decline in deforestation.

SKILLS PRACTICE

1 Change as a key concept (idea)

Try to find an example of the following ideas about change.

- Change involves any alteration to the natural environment.
- Change happens at varying rates.
- Change happens at different times.
- Change can be predictable.
- Change can be unpredictable.
- Change can bring about further change.

ISBN: 9780170418409

2 Naming items on a graph

a List the items that fit together to create the graph.

b State the pattern that the graph shows.

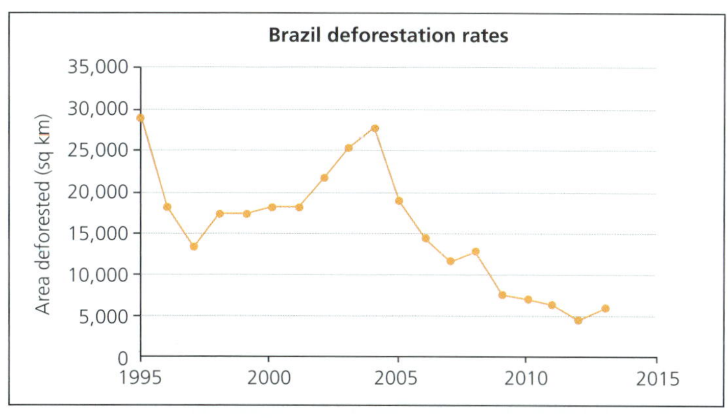

3 Creating a chart

Make a chart to show all the groups involved in reducing deforestation in Brazil and their actions.

4 Map drawing from an aerial photograph

An oblique view is taken at an angle, whereas a vertical view is taken straight down.

a State what view this is and why.

b Draw a sketch map of it to show the main features.

5 Comparing

State how Brazil's Amazonia is different to forest found in New Zealand.

Palm oil issue heats up

Palm oil is the most widely used edible oil on the planet and is found in about half of household products, from pizza to toothpaste to biofuel. **Some Kiwi farmers use palm kernel, a by-product of palm oil production and known as PKE, as a feed for cattle.**

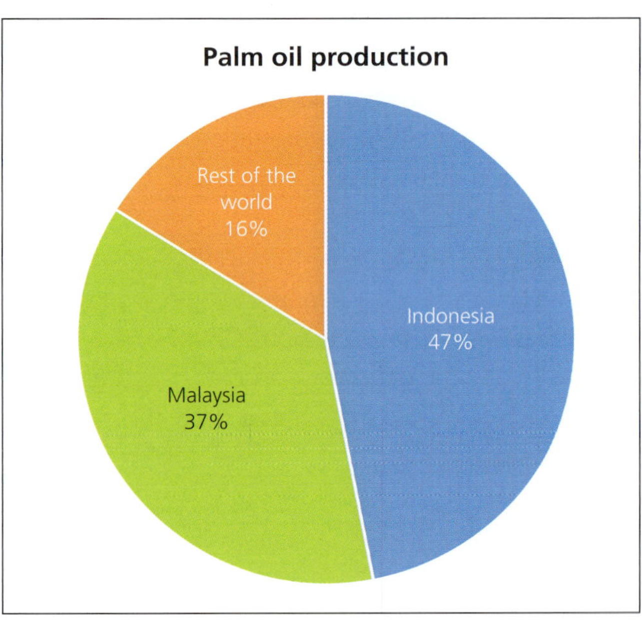

The palm oil production process

ISBN: 9780170418409

The issue

- Oil palms need a rainforest climate and a lot of land.
- To grow them, people get rid of rainforest and carbon-rich peatlands.
- This contributes to global warming and climate change by releasing carbon dioxide greenhouse gas into the atmosphere.
- It also takes away the habitat of animals including the orangutan, tiger and rhinoceros. Roading for palm oil plantations gives better access for poachers and wildlife smugglers.
- Therefore, much of the palm oil produced is unsustainable.

What is being done

1 An organisation called the Roundtable on Sustainable Palm Oil has set up international standards for sustainable palm oil production, although it does not ban deforestation.

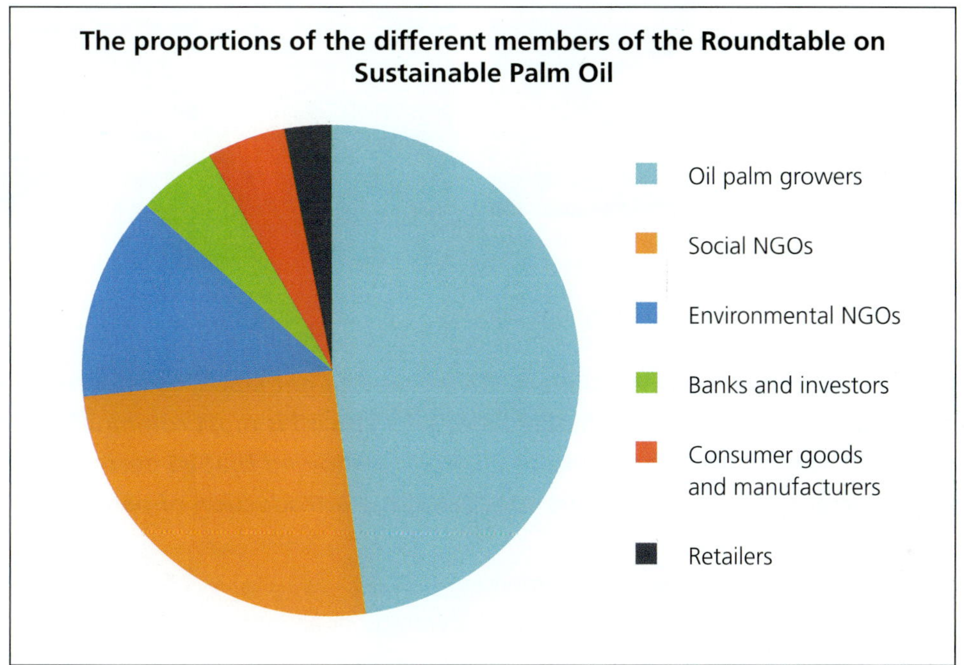

2 Leading firms such as Cargill have committed to cutting their ties to palm oil grown on deforested rainforest and peatland.

3 Governments are beginning to take notice of protests about the damage that growing oil palms can do to the environment. In April 2017, Indonesia held the first international conference on its sustainable palm oil scheme. The EU had been using palm oil for biofuels but it wanted to phase out the use of biofuels based on vegetable oils by 2020 because so much palm oil production was unsustainable.

4 Experts suggest there is enough non-forested land on which to put oil palm plantations. People have cleared rainforest to make cattle ranches but this land is run-down. Oil palm plantations on it would provide more jobs and money for locals than the cattle ranching, and palm trees, though not nearly as good as rainforest, at least absorb more carbon dioxide than cattle pasture does.

5 A country such as Brazil could produce large amounts of sustainably produced palm oil, which would be more popular than non-sustainably produced oil. This would pressure other countries such as Indonesia and Malaysia to go sustainable too.

6 Big Kiwi farming company Landcorp said it would stop using PKE because of the sustainability issue.

SKILLS PRACTICE

1 Flow chart

Use the photos on page 32 to show the steps of the process from deforestation to a bottle of palm oil.

2 Aerial views

One of these views is vertical and one is oblique. State which is which, and ways they differ in showing their subjects.

3 Evaluating an action

Read the following and answer the questions about it.

The Australasian campaign Unmask Palm Oil worked to get labelling of palm oil so that consumers could demand sustainable palm oil. Palm oil is most commonly labelled as 'vegetable oil', which can be any kind of oil. Polling showed that 85 percent of Australians and 92 percent of New Zealanders supported the introduction of palm oil labelling.

a State how the action could help the environment.

b State how the action, in your opinion, compares with other actions to make palm oil sustainable.

4 Seeing connections

While the use of biofuels is growing rapidly as an alternative to fossil fuels, some countries have restricted or excluded palm oil-based biofuels.

State why this is so and how oil palm growers could change that.

5 Graph format

a For the two graphs (pages 32 and 33) together supply the following.

- **i** A name for the type of graph and a description of how it works.
- **ii** A reason why the format is suitable to the content.

b For each of the graphs supply the following.

- **i** A more interesting title.
- **ii** A description of what it shows.

ISBN: 9780170418409

Environment and business can be mates

Old thinking = Human survival was linked with the economy, which made the world turn round and provided money for food and shelter.

New thinking = Human survival is linked with the economy *and* with the environment because a ruined environment means a ruined economy.

In the past = Economic companies topped the list of global polluters.

Compare with today

One Percent for the Planet is an international organisation of businesses that want to protect the natural environment. Members give at least one percent of annual sales to environmental causes. One of its founders was the founder of Patagonia, an American clothing company selling mainly sustainable outdoor clothes. Patagonia says it recognises that as a company that uses resources and produces waste, it impacts on the environment, and so feels a responsibility to give back. It donates in cash to thousands of community groups working to get positive change for the planet, in actions such as restoring forests and rivers, finding solutions to climate change, supporting sustainable agriculture and protecting habitats and plants and animals.

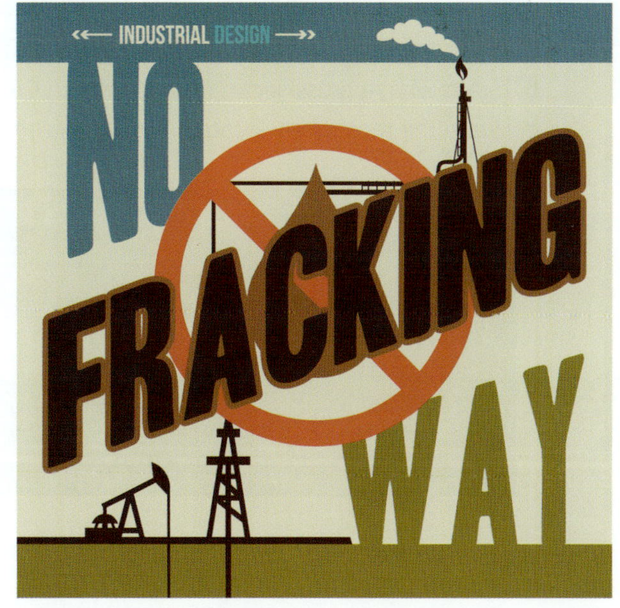

Examples of special projects partnerships

Ecotricity, one of Britain's biggest renewable energy companies, teamed up with Friends of the Earth, an international network of environmental organisations, which campaigns against fracking in the UK. Ecotricity's competitor, British Gas, had invested in fracking, which was the controversial process of injecting liquid at high pressure into existing fractures of underground rocks to extract oil or gas.

In May 2017, it was announced that the Auckland Harbour Bridge was to become the first major bridge in the world to have all its lighting powered entirely by solar power. The $10 million project was part of a 10-year energy efficiency partnership between power company Vector, which said it showed the company's commitment to sustainable energy, and Auckland Council, whose Mayor said it showed commitment as a city to energy efficiency, sustainability and low-carbon emissions.

- Rare blue duck (whio) found only in New Zealand. Features on the $10 note.
- Relies on fast-flowing and clean river water, which makes it a key indicator of how healthy a river is.
- In danger of becoming extinct because of habitat loss such as irrigation changing a river, and predators such as stoats.
- Many groups, such as kayaking and rafting companies, hunters, tangata whenua and environmental organisations, are involved in helping to save it.

Whio Forever Project is a partnership of Genesis Energy, which operates the Tongariro Power Scheme in the central North Island, and DOC. The project is about protecting populations of whio and encouraging the community to help. Funding from Genesis Energy allowed DOC to trap predators and double the number of whio recovery sites. DOC worked with Genesis Energy on an online game, Whio Boot Camp, in which players, as fledgling whio, had to collect flies and evade stoats in order to survive.

SKILLS PRACTICE

1 Cross-section

To generate power, the Tongariro Power Scheme uses water flowing from four rivers. Water passes through two power stations and ends up in a lake.

- **a** State the names of one river, the power stations, and the lake.
- **b** State what a cross-section is and why this is a cross-section.
- **c** State the most likely location for whio.

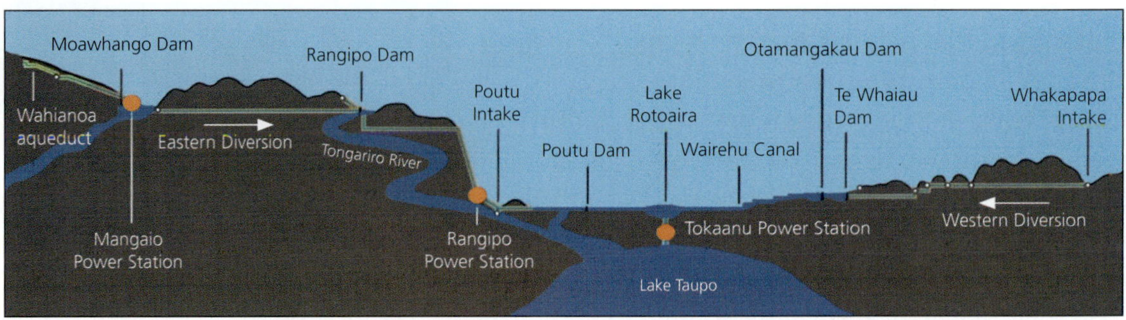

ISBN: 9780170418409

2 Infographic

Look at the fracking infographic below and state the following.

a What an infographic is.

b What the title suggests about possible bias (giving only one side).

c The purpose of using a cross-section in it.

d Whether you think the use of only a small amount of text is a good or a bad thing.

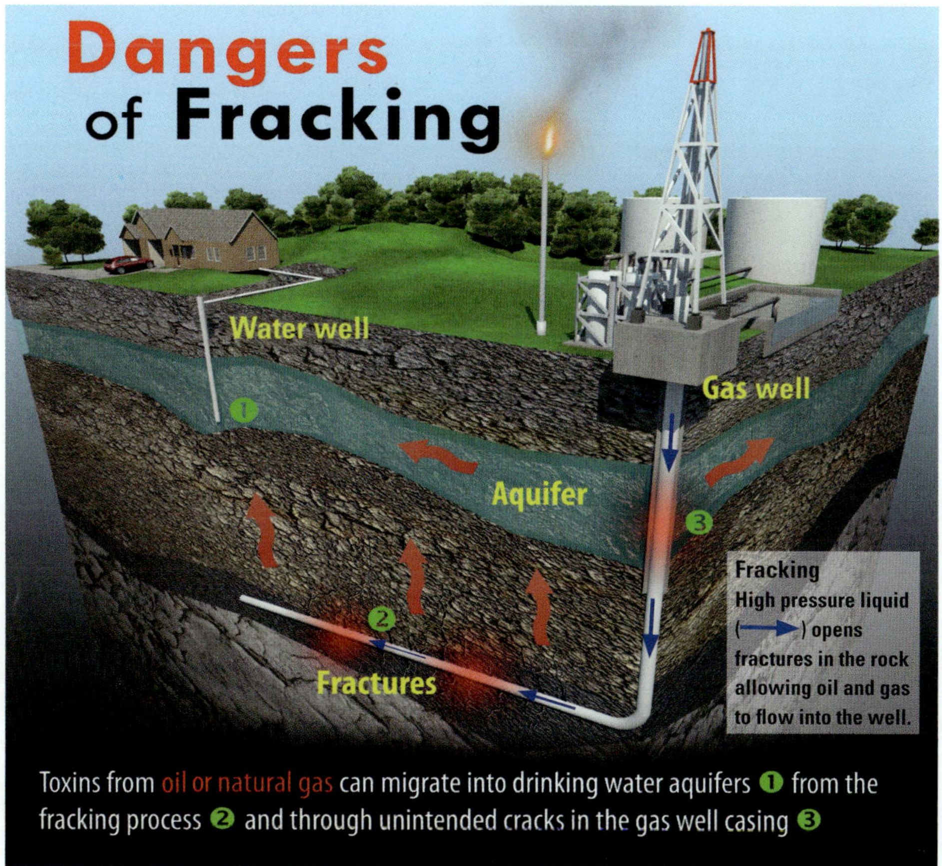

3 Understanding mutually beneficial relationships (both parties benefit)

State what each party gets out of the relationships mentioned in the text.

4 Surmising (thinking something is true without having evidence to prove it)

State what you surmise about the following.

a How the whio got its Maori and English names.

b What a fledgling whio is.

c Why whio can't be transferred to offshore islands to ensure their survival.

d Why business companies want to be recognised as environmentally responsible.

e Why fracking is controversial.

5 Understanding patterns (regular ways in which things are done)

a State the old pattern of behaviour of business towards the environment.

b State if this pattern is changing and, if so, how.

That humming sound is EVs

Electric vehicles (EVs).

- Can be powered solely by electric batteries or combinations.
- When driven, release no tailpipe air pollutants.
- Becoming more popular with today's focus on renewable energy.

In May 2016, the New Zealand Government announced an Electric Vehicles Programme, which included:

- a target of doubling the number of electric vehicles every year to reach about 64,000 by 2021
- $1 million annually for a nationwide electric vehicle information and promotion campaign over five years
- a fund to encourage and support innovative low-emission vehicle projects
- setting up an electric vehicles leadership group
- addressing barriers to the uptake of electric vehicles, such as the lack of awareness, and misunderstandings.

At that time:

- about 20 percent of New Zealand's greenhouse gas emissions was from transport
- 89 percent of that was from road transport
- emissions from the transport sector were projected to be 75 percent above 1990 levels by 2020
- the Ministry of Transport modelling indicated that doubling the uptake rate of electric/hybrid vehicles over the next 25 years could reduce emissions by 7 percent in the transport sector by 2040.

In 2017, 15 projects were conditionally approved to receive funding from the Low Emission Vehicles Contestable Fund. They included the use of 100 percent electric delivery vans, a car-share scheme using electric vehicles, an electric taxi fleet trial, two electric bus trials, and a facility to convert heavy vehicles to electric power.

Reasons people give for saying EVs are good for New Zealand:

- EVs use wasted energy by charging their main battery when braking.
- New Zealand's 230-volt electricity system means homes can charge them.
- 85 percent of homes have off-street parking, which allows overnight charging.
- Lessen reliance on fossil fuel.
- Reduce greenhouse gas emissions.
- Use clean, green, locally produced energy.
- Travel the Kiwi average daily driving distance without recharging.
- Cheaper to run than petrol or diesel vehicles.
- Contribute to the change to a low-carbon economy.
- Over 80 percent of New Zealand's electricity is generated from renewable sources.
- New Zealand has a target for 90 percent renewable electricity generation by 2025.

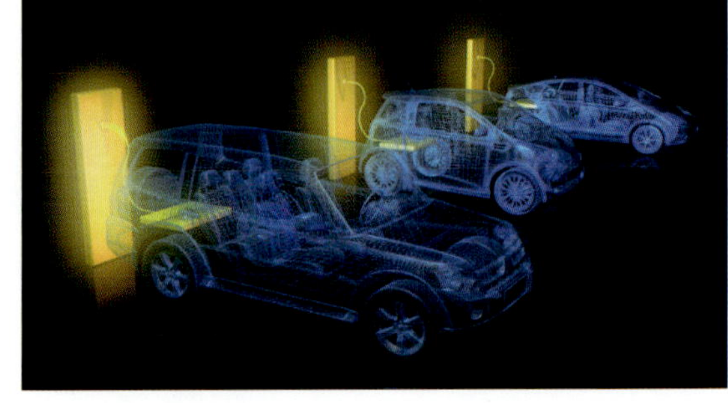

ISBN: 9780170418409

SKILLS PRACTICE

1 Analysis of a historic image

In Russia's St Petersburg, every winter from 1895 to 1910, electric tramways were laid on the frozen Neva River, connecting the Winter Palace area to an island. Power was supplied through the rails and a top cable supported by wooden piles. Trams ran at 20 kph and could carry 20 passengers per carriage. The carriages were converted from horse-cars.

a State how you can see the image is well over a hundred years old.

b State things you can observe (see) and things you can infer (make an educated guess from evidence).

2 Predicting

State how you see the future for each form of transport.

3 Explaining how something works

Explain how the mechanism works.

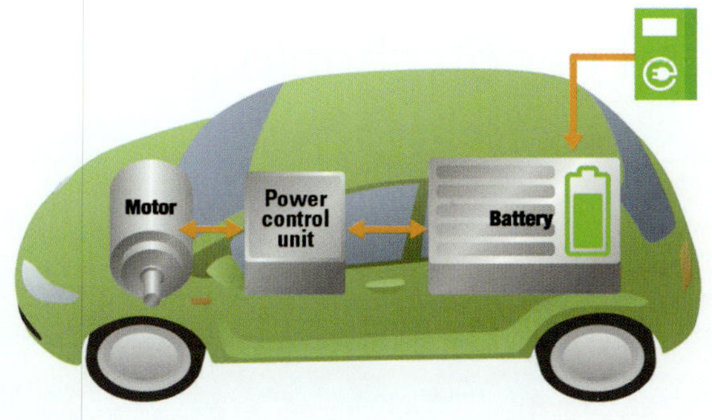

4 Personal opinion

a State what you would need to do to qualify for this parking space.

b State whether or not you would want to qualify for it and give reasons.

5 Distinguishing between fact and opinion (something you can prove and which is true and something that you think but can't prove)

State whether each of the following is a fact or an opinion and give a reason why.

a People who say EVs are the way of the future are nutters.

b The New Zealand Government announced an Electric Vehicles Programme.

c The New Zealand Government's announcement of an Electric Vehicles Programme showed lack of judgement.

d EVs will probably end up doing more damage to the environment than anything else we've had.

e The Low Emission Vehicles Contestable Fund was set up by the government.

ISBN: 9780170418409

Nanotechnology proposing a clean world

Nanotechnology:

- is a gigantic global lab where scientists explore matter on a scale 80,000 times smaller than a human hair
- could be the key to battling Earth's environmental problems by saving raw materials, energy and water, and by reducing greenhouse gases and hazardous wastes.

For something so little, it is a big ask.

Clean up past environmental damage.
Solve present environmental problems.
Prevent future environmental impacts.
Help sustain the planet for future generations.

Nano enthusiasts say,
'Bring it on.'

Examples of possible environmental nanotechnology

Microscopic nanorobots (nanobots) in the atmosphere as molecular scrubbers to deconstruct pollution molecules and make them harmless.

Nanoparticles added to material to reduce weight and save energy during transport.

Nanotechnology-based dirt- and water-resistant coatings to reduce cleaning.

Nanotechnology making battery recycling economic.

Nanomaterials for radioactive waste clean-up in water.

Nanotechnology-based solutions for oil spills.

Nanorobots swimming through water and eating polluting chemicals.

Iron nanoparticles cleaning up organic solvents polluting groundwater.

Nanotechnology water-purification devices to transform desalination.

Nano solar cells making solar power cheaper and more efficient by capturing the sun's infrared rays.

Using nanowires to construct cheaper and more efficient solar cells.

Nanotechnology cleaning up the hydrogen car.

Adding cerium oxide in nano form to diesel fuel to make it more efficient and emission-cleaning.

Nanoparticles removing toxic materials from gases.

ISBN: 9780170418409

Researchers agree that the safest possible future for advancing nanotechnology in a sustainable world can be reached by using green chemistry. Green chemistry means designing chemical products and processes in a way that reduces or gets rid of hazardous substances from the beginning to end of a chemical product's life cycle. Researchers also agree that nanotechnology can have side effects, and so risk assessments will be necessary for the impact on the environment and on human health.

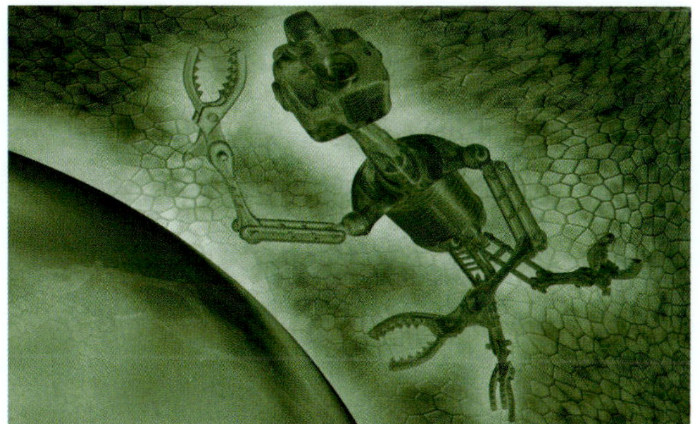

SKILLS PRACTICE

1 Making a pie chart

Make a pie chart to show the percentages for publication of nanotechnology articles in a recent year.

52.3% Asia and Oceania, 28.4% Europe, 14.7% North America, 2.7% Latin America, 1.9% Africa

2 Decision-making

NanoCamp is a camp delving into nanoscience and nanotechnology. Selected Year 12 and Year 13 students with a demonstrated interest in science have a week of residential lab experience with top scientists, completing hands-on investigations into various topics including electron microscopy, laser physics and nano-electronics, with postgraduate students providing day-to-day mentoring.

You are in Year 12 and your closest university is offering a NanoCamp. Decide if you would apply or not. Explain your decision.

3 Explaining a visual

Explain what the visual on the right is showing by referring to the written parts of it.

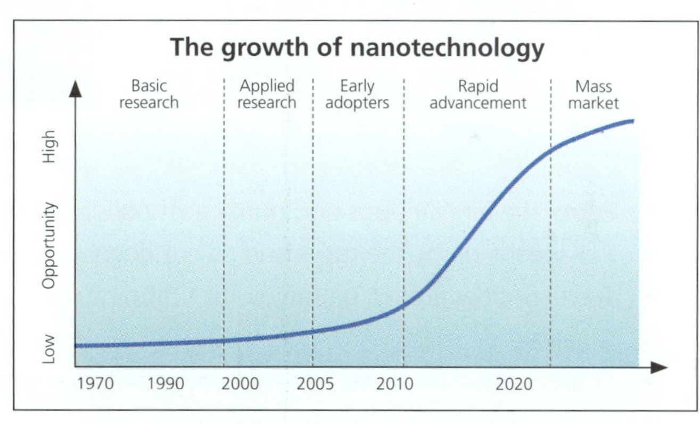

4 Making an unbiased presentation

Biased	Unbiased
All good	Good
or	*and*
All bad	Bad

You are to deliver a presentation on nanotechnology's possible role in helping to solve environmental problems. State what you should do to make sure it is unbiased.

5 Judging possibility

Read the following and answer the questions.

One day a personal nanofactory might sit on a desk in your house. As a 3D printer for atoms, it will be packed with miniature processors, computing and robotics, and let you make just about anything quickly, cleanly and cheaply.

a Do you think this is a real possibility? Give a reason for your answer.

b What impact on the environment might nanofactories have?

Robots gearing up to do battle for the environment

Robots are helping scientists understand and fight environmental threats such as pollution and global warming. Some of the following examples of robotic environmental work are already in operation and some are still in design. One way to ensure robots have little or no impact on the environment is to build them from biodegradable materials so they decompose into the earth once they have carried out their functions.

- Patrol the air like bugs and purify it of polluting materials.
- Pull weeds up by the roots and so cut down on herbicides.
- Travel underwater to gauge global warming, pollution and fishing issues.
- Clean up oil spills.
- Separate specific items from conveyor belts for recycling.
- Collect data from dangerous locations.
- Truck through human waste, using harnessed solar energy to help dry sewage, turning it and aerating it to keep down carbon emissions.
- Use soft tentacles to dance into delicate environments such as coral reefs to find data for scientists.
- Blast seawater into the air to form low-level cloud cover to reflect more solar radiation.
- Act as human proxies at remote locations and so save aviation fuel.
- Rid the ocean of plastics.
- Clean solar panels with less water than standard methods.
- Use legs to get over forest obstacles such as rocks and fallen trees and fireproof armour to fight fires. Use four arms and huge blades to clear trees to make a firebreak.
- Use a sonic emitter to drive marine wildlife away from oil spills.
- Look for biomass to eat and get its energy from.
- Running on methanol fuel cell, with GPS navigation, use digital image recognition to distinguish plant and weed, and use rotating tool to cut weeds.

ISBN: 9780170418409

The Fukushima Daiichi nuclear power plant meltdown in 2011 in Japan left radioactive rubbish. Radiation levels were higher than humans could survive, so engineers built scorpion robots with cameras attached to see the damage. Early robots helped give information such as the situation around damaged reactors. Later robots were to swim through underwater tunnels of cooling pools and remove blobs of melted fuel rods. In 2017, the robots sent in were 'dying' because the high amounts of leaked radioactive materials destroyed their wiring. The government estimated the clean-up of the environment could take decades, with continued help from robots or with some new technology.

SKILLS PRACTICE

1 Designing

You are designing a robot. Give it a name, state how it will help the environment, and state how you have ensured it is the most environmentally-friendly robot possible.

2 Finding examples

For each of the following about robots, give an example.

- **a** Not being fit for purpose
- **b** Useful for firefighting
- **c** Useful for environmental monitoring
- **d** Useful for agriculture
- **e** Useful to fight oil spill damage
- **f** Useful in sewage treatment

3 Future problem-solving

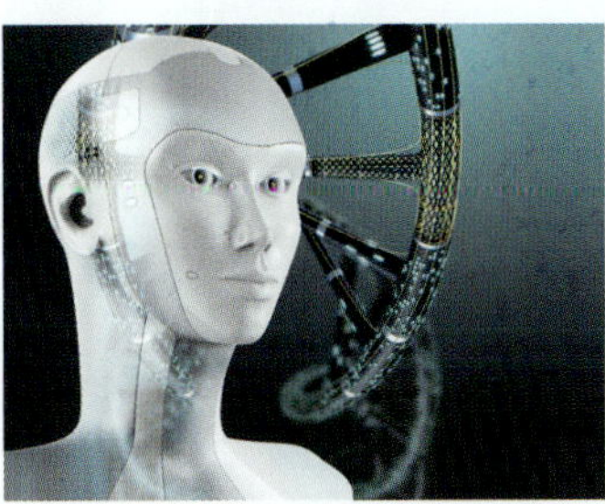

It is possible that not only will robots clean up the environment, they will also use artificial intelligence (AI) to create solutions to environmental problems. (AI = able to do tasks normally needing human intelligence such as visual recognition and decision-making.)

Name three environmental problems you would want such robots to look at first. Say why you chose them.

4 Sentence construction (simple and clear is a good start)

The world has the technology for clean energy to help stop global warming. Write a few sentences about how robots might help in this area.

5 Understanding personification (giving human characteristics to something that is non-human)

An explosion at the Pike River coal mine on the West Coast of the South Island in November 2010 killed 29 men. The government said gas levels made it too dangerous to re-enter the mine to retrieve the bodies but a number of robots with cameras were sent in in the following years.

Study the cartoon and work out how and why the cartoonist has used personification.

ISBN: 9780170418409

Creative thinkers spring into action

Creative thinkers:

- look at problems from a fresh angle that suggests novel solutions
- are open-minded and flexible
- are risk-takers and good communicators
- can see the full picture.

Students of today operate in a society of fast change. They will need creative skills to solve global environmental problems.

One method

Step 1: Think of the current situation, e.g. countries still using fossil fuels.

Step 2: Think of the future, e.g. fossil fuels stay in the ground.

Step 3: Think of making bridges from present to future, e.g. bridge to fossil-fuel-free made up of about 200 boards with the name of a different country on each one …

Examples of creative thinking

Some New Zealand farmers are trying out new crops such as lavender, tea, saffron, macadamias and hazelnuts, and different seeds, to lower their carbon emissions.

Aquaflow, a company based in Nelson, was one of the first to suss out the technology needed to harvest wild algae from sewage ponds, and then extract fuel from it that was suitable for cars and aircraft.

Gull has a biodiesel that comes from oils from fish and chip shops. It also makes bioethanol from waste products from the making of beer and milk.

Z Company has New Zealand's first biodiesel plant — in Wiri in Auckland. Its Z Bio D is made from inedible tallow, a fatty substance from rendered (melted down) animal fat and a by-product of the Kiwi agricultural industry. It reduces carbon emissions, as it burns more cleanly than ordinary diesel, and is locally sourced.

ISBN: 9780170418409

The Sustainable Business Network has a vision to make New Zealand the model sustainable nation for the world and for New Zealand to be self-sufficient by 2050 with all its energy coming from renewable sources. It published a report on Business Opportunities for a Sustainable New Zealand, which was bursting with creative ideas. Examples included: creating a set-up pack and a website platform to let consumers offer their driveways for electric vehicle charging stations; building a demonstration home with technology of the future such as onsite solar energy generation, and showing how electric vehicles fit in with the home; running a campaign on biofuels to bust myths about them; using smartphone devices such as apps to help people plan trips on public transport; and a free-ride challenge where people get free access to public transport services for a day to encourage them to keep using it.

Creative thinking can become part of a country's culture. For example, Thailand is looking for green technologies and its creative solutions range from a domestic sugar producer powering processing plants with steam turbines that run on burned leftover sugarcane waste, to using new material sciences that produce biodegradable plastics from local sugarcane feedstock.

SKILLS PRACTICE

1 **Summarising** (showing main points only)

a Write a summary of what the visual below shows.

b Write a summary of what creative thinkers, trying to solve environmental problems, would like a similar graph for 2025 to look like.

c Write a summary of no more than one sentence for why a global energy consumption visual for 2017 has data from two years ago.

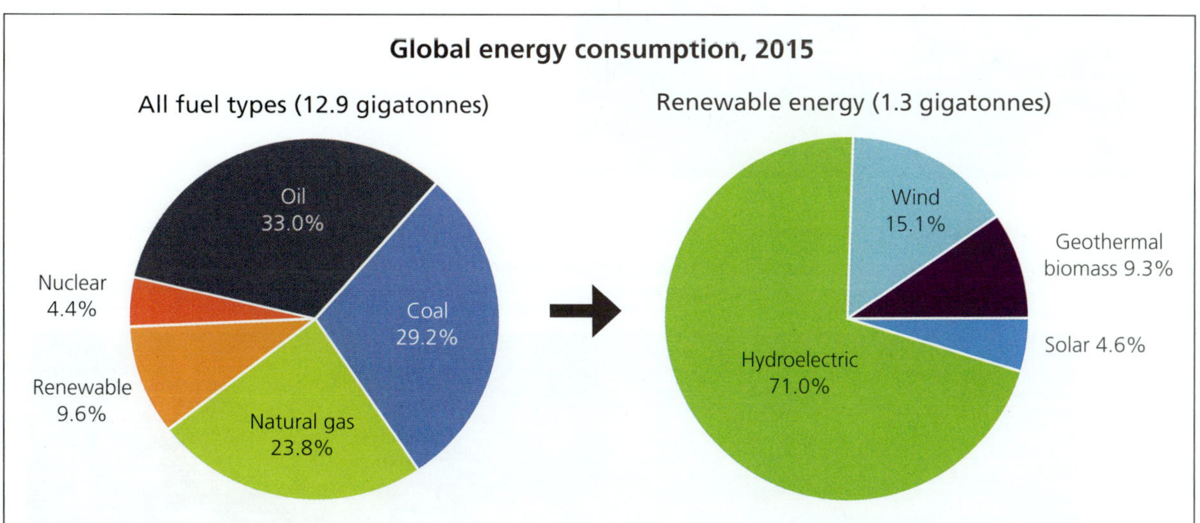

2 **Understanding zines** (self-published texts and images with small circulation by individuals or small groups)

Example = zine using computerese (computer language) about disposing of your computer and electronics in an environmentally-friendly way.

List some ideas you could suggest to your group, which has been tasked with producing a zine using ideas from this unit.

ISBN: 9780170418409

3 **Conceptualising** (forming a concept or idea)

A member of your team has suggested this for your environmental company's redesigned website. State your opinion about its suitability.

4 **Focusing**

a State what the image means.

b State why focusing is important for creative thinkers.

c Assess your own ability to focus.

5 **Being optimistic**

Read the following and state why creative thinkers need to be optimistic.

India, with over 1.3 billion people, is one of the world's most polluted countries. By 2016, its capital city, New Delhi, had about 20 million people and 10 million cars. India's target was that only electric cars would be operating there by 2030. At that time there was only one Indian company making EVs.

ISBN: 9780170418409

Clicktivism makes the environment go viral

18

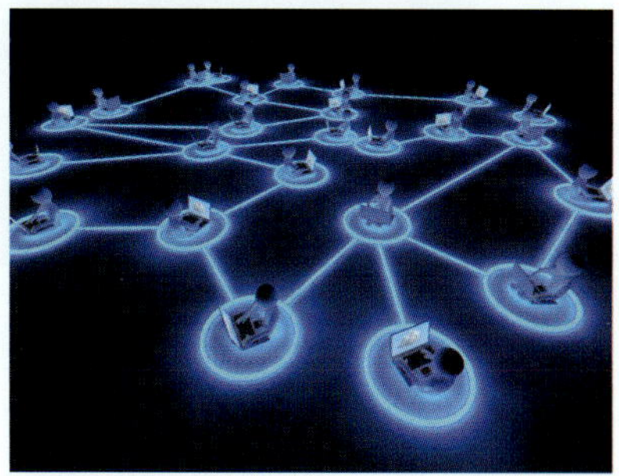

Chats, forums, wikis, microblogging, rating, video, podcasts, weblogs, bookmarking ... None of these was available to early environmentalists. Nor were any of the following examples of social media:

Bebo (2005), Blogger (1999), Digg (2004), Facebook (2004), Flickr (2004), Google (1998), Instagram (2010), LinkedIn (2002), LiveJournal (1999), Myspace (2003), Periscope (2015), Pinterest (2010), Reddit (2005), Skype (2003), Snapchat (2011), Tumblr (2007), Twitter (2006), Vimeo (2004), Wikia (2004), Wikipedia (2001), YouTube (2005).

The environmental sector is using social media to ...

- support environmental campaigns.
- spread environmental messages, photos and petitions.
- try to influence government decisions on environmental issues.
- connect people around the world on issues such as climate change.
- let ordinary people share local data such as air and water quality.
- give reports on unfolding events such as oil spills.
- use geolocation and hashtags to share environmental stories.
- spread slogans such as *Do or Fry*; *Be Part of the Solution, Not the Pollution*.
- show leaders public feeling on environmental issues.
- let ordinary people be the source of creative ideas and plans.
- connect local environmental challenges and solutions to global ones.
- give people power to influence government decisions that affect everybody.
- let people feel as if they are involved and contributing.
- increase visibility and awareness of environmental issues.
- give government services ways to communicate with the public.
- let celebrities such as movie and pop stars encourage people to engage with issues.
- provide visual proof such as a company illegally discharging waste.
- let companies get instant publicity for environmentally-friendly efforts.
- let companies prove their environmentally-friendly efforts rather than just saying how good their environmental plans are.
- have one-to-one conversations with real people rather than an anonymous voice with the same message for everybody.
- provide instant information from visuals like infographics.

ISBN: 9780170418409

SKILLS PRACTICE

1 Photo sharing

a State how you use or could use social media to share photos.

b State how photos on social media is a powerful tool for the environmental fight-back.

2 Thinking backwards

You live in 1970 before clicktivism hit the globe. You have adopted an environmental cause and want to spread the word.

State what the cause is and the process you will follow to get your message out.

3 Using dates

a Look at the dates for the examples of social media (page 47).

b State the most obvious pattern you can see.

c State if any popular social medium has been omitted and, if so, what it is and how it helps the environmental fight-back.

4 Role-playing

You have been appointed to a company as its Environmental Adviser and are to have your first board meeting to outline plans for greening the company. Make some notes on what you might say about whether or not the company should use social media.

5 Using idioms

An idiom is an expression whose meaning is different from what the individual words suggest. The idiom 'to bury your head in the sand' means to ignore or hide from danger. It comes from the mistaken belief that that is what an ostrich does.

a State what is happening in the image and how the image illustrates an idiom.

b State how you might use the idiom for an image about people denying the power of social media to help spread environmental messages.

ISBN: 9780170418409

Hopping on to existing platforms

19

Building on existing platforms can help get you up and going.

Example 1: Green Cross International

Green Cross International is:

- headquartered in Geneva in Switzerland
- built on a platform started by a 1992 Earth Summit held by the United Nations to talk about issues such as alternatives for fossil fuels
- built on the response model of Red Cross so it can respond to environmental issues and work for solutions.

The Green Cross International Charter states: '… As the issues of climate change and environmental degradation bring about a much needed wake-up call to modern society with the realisation that the global challenges of security, poverty and the environment are intrinsically connected, Green Cross International will focus its activities on this critical nexus [connection] in the quest for a just, secure and sustainable future for humanity.'

For example, it has programmes to:

- get cooperation between countries that share rivers
- clean up pollution such as dumped pesticides and nuclear waste
- get people to change behaviours and values towards the environment
- get a sustainable energy future
- analyse the environmental impact of wars and conflicts
- safely destroy stockpiles of conventional and chemical weapons.

Example 2: Miss Earth

The Miss Earth Pageant:

- aims to promote environmental awareness
- is an annual and global competition on beauty and knowledge of environmental issues
- was built on the platform of the beauty pageant entertainment industry
- calls the winner Miss Earth and the runners-up Miss Fire, Miss Air and Miss Water
- has its winner act as ambassador to environmental campaigns worldwide such as tree planting, coastal clean-ups, and media guesting.

Its Miss Earth Foundation focuses on educating young people in environmental awareness. Its major project, I Love Planet Earth School Tour, teaches school children and distributes educational aids.

Its Miss Earth Eco-Fashion Design Competition is an annual event for eco-friendly designs such as those made from recyclable and natural materials.

Its Miss Earth Declaration says it should be everybody's agenda to make Earth smile again.

Example 3: Young Champions of the Earth

In 2017, the United Nations Environment Programme launched Young Champions of the Earth to celebrate and support people between the ages of 18 and 30 who have a great chance of having a positive impact on the environment. After a global jury chooses winners, the UN names six people each year as Young Champions of the Earth (one from each global region — Africa, Asia-Pacific, Europe, Latin America and the Caribbean, North America, and West Asia).

The winners' packages include:

- US$15,000 in seed funding
- training to help kickstart their ideas
- a week-long entrepreneurship boot-camp (all expenses paid)
- mentoring to help bring their environmental ideas to life
- attendance at the UN Environment Assembly in Nairobi and the UN General Assembly in New York (all expenses paid)
- introductions to over 100 environment ministers at the Champions of the Earth Gala Dinner
- publicity and recognition through online and global media.

SKILLS PRACTICE

1 Logo designing

a Sketch out a design for a logo to identify Green Cross International and another for Miss Earth.

b Find copies of the actual logos and compare them with your sketches.

c State which logos you prefer and why.

2 Understanding terminology

Green Cross International says it seeks solutions through dialogue, mediation and cooperation. Show what these three things mean by any method you like, for example drawing, writing, …

3 Personal assessment of values and strengths

State which you would rather win: an Olympic gold medal, Young Champion of the Earth, the Man Booker Prize (for fiction writing), a Grammy Award, or an Oscar. Give reasons for your answer and say how your decision reflects your values and strengths.

4 Preparing an answer

Read these examples of Miss Earth questions and then choose one of them. Prepare an answer to it.

- How can we improve the environment and get others more involved?
- What is the most important environmental issue and how can we fix it?
- Has our generation helped or hurt the environment? How?
- How have you helped the environment?
- If you had the chance to talk to the whole world, what would you say?

5 Using prior knowledge

Green Cross International, Miss Earth and Young Champions of the Earth build on existing platforms. Explain that statement in either words or diagrams.

ISBN: 9780170418409

Groups get going

Group = collection of people who are classed together or considered to be a unit
= formal or informal.

	Formal	Informal
Structure	Defined	Loose
Roles	Clearly defined responsibilities	No real defined responsibilities
Leadership	Appointed by a set process	If any, emerge naturally
Reason for	Deliberately for specific task	Voluntarily for non-specific activities
Membership	Depends on rules	Join and leave whenever desired
Importance	Given to positions	Given to people
Communication	Along set lines	In any direction
Relationships	Professional	Personal

Examples

The World Future Council is a group of 50 leading global change-makers with their eye on the future who come together to consult and discuss solutions that help sustainable development. Its environmental working areas include renewable energy, regenerative cities (urban areas looking after their environments), and preserving forests, biodiversity, oceans and coasts.

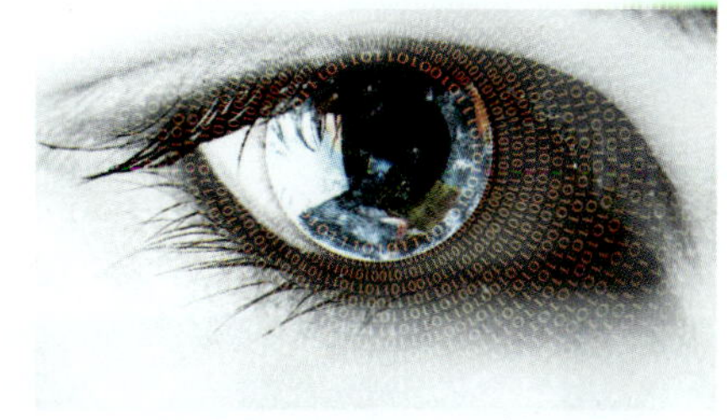

Enviroschools Kaupapa (Maori for vision, ideas, and plan) is about making a healthy, peaceful and sustainable world where people work with and learn from nature. Examples are: planting trees pupils have grown themselves; finding different ways such as aquaponics to grow food in a cold place with poor soil; problem-solving the issue of waste by creating toys out of recycled items and building huts of natural materials; creating habitats for insects; taking a garden to the Ellerslie International Flower Show; building an outdoor classroom; and building a Living Room.

Community gardens are run by groups who garden a piece of land together and add environmental benefits to an urban area by restoring oxygen to the air and reducing air pollution, filtering rainwater to help keep groundwater clean, recycling by composting, reducing food miles and greenhouse emissions from transporting food, reducing packaging and chemical preservatives and pesticides, planting heirloom species, and transforming wasteland into productive areas.

ISBN: 9780170418409

Waipoua Forest Trust is located in Northland where it is involved in restoring the Waipoua Forest area to a turangawaewae o kauri, a place where kauri can stand. In partnership with Te Roroa iwi, the Maori guardians of Waipoua, it helps guide DOC in its management role.

Scientists are a group of experts who study the environment and how it affects plants and animals, and who can also develop plans to fix environmental problems. They are always finding out something new about the environment. One example is their idea of de-extinction, which means bringing back to life extinct species like the moa. Another example is research that shows New Zealand actually sits on a continent called Zealandia, which covers about five million square kilometres, of which 94 percent is under water. No body exists to declare Zealandia a continent but it is increasingly being referred to as such in scientific literature.

The public, or the community, is an informal group and it breaks into smaller groups who share the same opinions about particular environmental issues. An example is deep-sea oil drilling in New Zealand. The group in favour of drilling says oil is a resource that can be used to get money and will benefit the economy. The risks to the environment are small because before operators even begin exploring, they have to prove they can work to very high safety and environmental standards. The group against drilling says it risks environmentally damaging oil spills, that the world must move away from oil because of climate change, that getting oil from the ocean floor brings up toxic substances like mercury, lead and arsenic that are often released back into the ocean, that it creates waste such as bilge water, and that sound waves used to locate oil can harm sea mammals and disorientate whales.

SKILLS PRACTICE

1 Expanding

Expand the chart on differences between formal and informal groups (page 51) by adding other points and by using examples.

2 Choosing either/or

Either compare and contrast the two posters, or create your own poster for or against deep-sea drilling.

ISBN: 9780170418409

3 Understanding how visuals illustrate ideas

State how this cartoon illustrates the idea that groups may conflict over the use of resources.

4 Understanding Maori concepts

aroha love, sympathy
kaitiakitanga caring for the environment
mana whenua right to manage land
tikanga Maori customs and traditions
mana respect
iwi tribe
taonga treasure
mauri life force

State how one or more of the concepts are linked to one or more of the groups mentioned.

5 Considering a new finding

State why Zealandia shows that ideas about the environment can change.

21

Film-makers can blow your mind

Many people report how it was a film that got them thinking about and involved in issues such as climate change.

Examples of movies with environmental ideas:

- ***Blade Runner***, 1982. Rainy climate of a changed Los Angeles.
- ***Split Second***, 1992. Flooded London.
- ***Waterworld***, 1995. Future world almost all covered with water.
- ***The Day After Tomorrow***, 2004. Catastropic climate effects as a result of global warming.
- ***Avatar***, 2009. Battle to save a moon from mining by humans in 2154.
- ***The Age of Stupid***, 2009. A man alone in a wrecked world of 2055 watches footage from 2008 and asks, Why didn't we stop climate change when we had the chance?
- ***Beasts of the Southern Wild***, 2012. Rising seas.

- ***Snowpiercer***, 2014. Botched climate engineering has plunged Earth into a new ice age and the only survivors are in a train that circumnavigates the globe.
- ***Climate Change Denial Disorder***, 2015. CCDD is a disease that attacks the brain, leaving the person unable to understand words related to climate change such as 'factual' and 'melting'. People are urged to help politicians suffering from it.

Examples of documentaries with environmental ideas:

- ***Garbage Warrior***, 2008. Fight by eco architect to build off-the-grid self-sufficient communities.
- ***Lessons of the Loess Plateau***, 2009. Large-scale environmental restoration project by the Chinese Government and the World Bank in China's northern area.
- ***Carbon Nation***, 2010. Ways in which the energy Earth consumes can be met while reducing or getting rid of carbon-based sources.
- ***Climate of Change***, 2010. Ordinary people around the world making a difference in the fight against global warming.
- ***Earth: The Operators' Manual***, 2011. Climate change and sustainable energy solutions.
- ***The Cleantech Future***, 2012. Possibilities of a new industrial revolution through cleantech entrepreneurship and corporate practices.
- ***The Fight for Amazonia***, 2012. Efforts to save the rainforest.
- ***Words from the Edge***, 2014. The change from industrial growth to more localised, sustainable, living economies.
- ***The True Cost***, 2015. Damage caused by the fast fashion industry.
- ***A Simpler Way: Crisis as Opportunity***, 2016. A community in Australia chooses a simpler life in response to global crisis.

ISBN: 9780170418409

- ***Before the Flood***, 2016. Movie star Leonardo DiCaprio on climate change and moving to a cleaner and greener future.
- ***The Breakthrough in Renewable Energy***, 2016. Inside the corporate offices and production lines with investment in renewable energy.

- ***An Inconvenient Truth***, 2006, the work of former US Vice-President Al Gore, won an Academy Award. Al Gore was joint winner of the 2007 Nobel Peace Prize, along with the United Nations Intergovernmental Panel on Climate Change.
- ***The Cove***, 2009, which showed the controversial killing of dolphins in a small Japanese coastal town, won an Oscar. Another nominee was *Food, Inc.*, which showed how agribusiness produced food in a way that harmed the environment.
- ***The Warriors of Qiugang: A Chinese Village Fights Back***, 2010, was one of four environmental documentaries nominated for Oscars. It was about villagers fighting companies that were polluting local rivers.

Filming uses a lot of energy such as caterers delivering food, flying actors and film crews, power plants providing electricity to studio lots. Some film-makers are trying to be environmentally-friendly. The director of *The Day after Tomorrow*, a movie where climate change causes environmental disasters around the world, tried to make sure production of the movie would not contribute to global warming. The *Matrix* sequels recycled just about all the material used in the building of sets. At the Vancouver Film Festival in 2016, four Sustainability Executives from major Hollywood studios took part in a forum on sustainable production. On the recent *X-Files* reboot, the series managed to recycle at least 80 percent of material waste. It enforced a no-idling policy and used biofuels and biodiesel whenever possible. NBCUniversal's Sustainability Director created their own LED lighting. Universal's *The Fast and the Furious* and Fox's *Wolverine 3* used solar-powered trailers. Warner Bros uses biodiesel across productions.

SKILLS PRACTICE

1 Using persuasion

As the Sustainability Director for a major Hollywood studio, state:

a how important you think your job is

b how you might use costs to help you win some battles such as getting stars to use their own coffee mugs instead of disposable ones and to eat local seasonal food.

2 Planning

Use one to make a plan for a short movie with an environmental theme.

3 Considering the 5Ws and H

State your considerations on the following.

How reality television has helped make documentary films popular.
What impact technology is having on making films more accessible to the public.
When you might expect to see James Bond driving environmentally-friendly vehicles and living sustainably.
Where a film-maker could film something in your community that is helping the environment.
Who among Hollywood stars is helping the environment.
Why film studios are embracing sustainability.

4 Improving

A take-away from these environmental films is that ordinary people can demand that politicians listen and change government policies on things such as climate change.

The image here is a studio shot. See if you can find a better image to illustrate people getting government to follow them.

5 Recommending

Recommend four films for a company to screen during a four-day workshop on environmental awareness. State why you would recommend them over others.

ISBN: 9780170418409

And the winner is ...

22

The growth of environmental awareness has led to an increasing number of awards around the world. For example, the Goldman Environmental Prize, known as the Green Nobel Prize, is the world's most famous award for environmental activism, where winners may be people who have worked undercover or risked their lives. Winners in 2017 included a Slovenian who got a polluting cement plant shut down, an Indian who rallied his tribe to stop a UK bauxite company mining sacred hills, a park ranger in the Democratic Republic of Congo who exposed corruption in a British oil company, and an Australian woman who stopped a multinational coal-mining company from taking her family farm and protected her community from further pollution.

The Kiwi Green Ribbon Awards of the Ministry for the Environment go to individuals, communities and organisations that have made outstanding contributions to protect and manage New Zealand's environment. Here are the 2017 winners of the 10 categories.

Caring for Our Water *and* the Supreme Award — Whangawehi Catchment Management Group Working as a community to help a local waterway by actions such as planting native trees, fencing, making dams to retain silt and build up stream beds, and trapping pests.

Protecting Our Biodiversity — Pirongia Te Aroaro o Kahu Restoration Society Working to bring kokako back after pests cut numbers and the last birds were sent to Tiritiri Matangi and Kapiti islands.

Protecting Our Coasts and Oceans — South Taranaki Underwater Diving Club Working to fill in gaps in information about the coastal marine area, by actions such as building and placing a camera on the reef floor, and citizen scientists including local school children volunteering to survey the images and document reef life.

Resilience to Climate Change — Port Nelson Working with local businesses to reduce transport emissions by increasing efficiency of road freight operations between wineries and port.

Business Leadership — Countdown (Progressive Enterprises) Working to stop food waste, such as diverting good-quality, edible food waste to its charity partners like foodbanks, and other food waste to farmers as cattle-feed.

Minimising Our Waste — Webstar Auckland magazine printing company recycling 99 percent of its solid waste through actions such as compressing paper dust into briquettes for composting, and on-selling used IBC containers.

Philanthropy and Partnership — Taranaki Mounga Project Ltd (Mounga is local spelling for maunga, mountain.) A partnership of Taranaki iwi, DOC, NEXT Foundation and the local community supported by sponsors working to restore Taranaki Mounga through actions such as installing the world's largest ever network of self-resetting rat traps.

Community Leadership — Banks Peninsula Conservation Trust With landowners, Christchurch City Council, DOC, and Environment Canterbury, working to protect the area through actions such as getting protection for a whole stream from summit through private farmland to the sea.

Kaitiaki Leadership — Lake Waiporohita Restoration Local iwi Ngati Kahu, with Northland Regional Council, DOC and Landcorp working to restore the lake through actions such as building fences and a barrier to stop stock and vehicle access, replacing non-native trees with natives, and creating a weir to settle sediment and nutrient coming from a farm.

Leadership in Communication and Education — Zealandia Wellington's eco-sanctuary running an environmental education programme for young people through actions such as the Zealandia trading card game and an app to record in-sanctuary learning experiences, and 10 Youth Ambassadors working alongside the education team.

SKILLS PRACTICE

1 Looking at purpose

State the general purpose of any awards.

State the specific purpose of the Green Ribbon Awards.

2 Locating

The numbers on the map at right refer to the specific locations featured in the Green Ribbon Awards. Match the numbers to the places.

3 Comparing and contrasting

List the features that the Green Ribbon winners had in common and the features they did not have in common.

4 Awarding

Like many countries, New Zealand is upping its awards for environmental work. For example, the Minister of Conservation awards the Loder Cup each year outstanding work in flora conservation.

State the name of an environmental award you would like to create, what form the award would be such as a trophy or cash, what the award would be for and why you would like people to enter.

5 Advertising

Create an advertisement for your local newsletter to alert people that entry forms for the Green Ribbon Awards are now available.

ISBN: 9780170418409

International positivism

The environment still struggles in many places. But, says the United Nations, let's have one day of the year dedicated to celebrating the world and all the positives going on for the environment.

The United Nations General Assembly made World Environment Day to commemorate the opening of the Stockholm Conference on the Human Environment.

On the same day, the General Assembly created the United Nations Environment Programme (UNEP), which is now the United Nations' main agency for environmental action.

UNEP is responsible, along with the World Meteorological Organization, for starting the IPCC, the international agency responsible for monitoring climate change.

Celebrated every year on 5 June.

Aims to raise awareness for environmental issues.

Is a global people's event.

Has a new theme and a new host country each year.

Gets people worldwide to think and act locally to protect their own communities.

All sorts of activities such as parades, street rallies, concerts, tree planting, recycling and community clean-ups.

Aims to be the biggest annual event for positive environmental action.

Empowers people to become active agents to fight for the environment.

Gets communities to see how important they are to changing attitudes.

ISBN: 9780170418409

New Zealand hosted World Environment Day in 2008. The theme was 'Kick the Habit! Towards a Low Carbon Economy'. At that time New Zealand was one of five countries worldwide to have pledged to become carbon neutral.

There are also many other special days for the environment including the following.

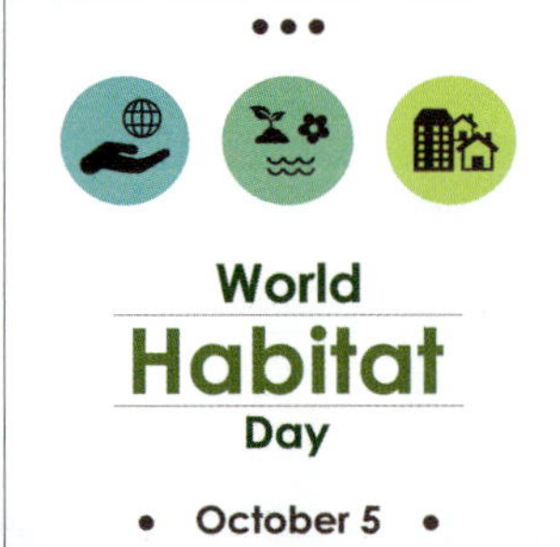

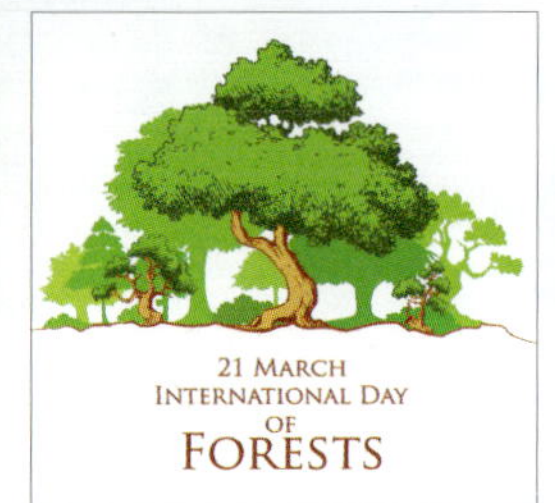

SKILLS PRACTICE

1 Recommending

Examples of themes and countries for World Environment Day include Wildlife (Angola, 2016), Consumption (Italy, 2015), Climate Change and Sea Level Rise (Barbados, 2014), Environmentally Sound Food Choices (Mongolia, 2013), Green Economy (Brazil, 2012), and Connecting People to Nature (Canada 2017). Recommend a good theme for next year and state which country you think should host it. Say why you recommend that theme and country.

2 Understanding acronyms (abbreviations formed from first letters of words and sometimes said as a word)

Work out what these acronyms stand for.

UN *WED* *IPCC* *UNEP* *WMO* *UNGA*

3 Recognising irony (the use of words that are strange or amusing because they are the opposite of what you might expect)

This 2008 cartoon refers to the Greens in New Zealand pointing out that Chapter 13, which said the effects of dairy waste on the environment were bad, was removed from the Report on the Environment.

State why the event depicted in the cartoon could be said to be ironic. (Clue = date.)

ISBN: 9780170418409

4 Captioning

These images all have the same theme of celebrating World Environment Day but captions for them need to be different.

Prepare captions for them.

5 Getting the message

Read the following extracts and list the main points.

a *Our dependence on carbon-based energy has caused a significant build-up of greenhouse gases in the atmosphere. Last year, the Nobel Peace Prize-winning Intergovernmental Panel on Climate Change put the final nail in the coffin of global-warming sceptics. We know that climate change is happening, and we know that carbon dioxide and other greenhouse gases that we emit are the cause.*

b *'Kick the Habit! Towards a Low Carbon Economy' recognises the damaging extent of our addiction, and it shows the way forward.*
Often we need a crisis to wake us to reality. With the climate crisis upon us, businesses and governments are realising that, far from costing the Earth, addressing global warming can actually save money and invigorate economies.

c *Even better news is that technologies already exist or are under development to make our consumption of carbon-based fuels cleaner and more efficient, and to harness the renewable power of sun, wind and waves. Around the world, nations, cities, organisations and businesses are looking afresh at green options.*

d *The message of World Environment Day 2008 is that we are all part of the solution. Whether you are an individual, an organisation, a business or a government, there are many steps you can take to reduce your carbon footprint. It is a message we all must take to heart.*
(UN Secretary-General's message for World Environment Day 2008)

Measuring the good and the bad

Protecting the environment is a common theme of the new United Nations Global Goals for Sustainable Development. There are 17 goals for the world to reach by 2030 and they cover issues such as fighting climate change and looking after forests and oceans.

The Environmental Performance Index tries to measure how countries are doing. It calculates 20 indicators in areas such as air quality, agriculture, climate and energy. The higher the overall score, the better the country has performed. The 2016 Environmental Performance Index ranked 180 countries.

Top 28 countries and score

Country	Score
Finland	90.88
Iceland	90.51
Sweden	90.43
Denmark	89.21
Slovenia	88.98
Spain	88.91
Portugal	88.63
Estonia	88.59
Malta	88.48
New Zealand	88.00
UK	87.38
Australia	87.22
Singapore	87.04
Croatia	86.98
Switzerland	86.93
Norway	86.90
Austria	86.64
Ireland	86.60
Luxembourg	86.58
Greece	85.81
Latvia	85.71
Lithuania	85.49
Slovakia	85.42
Canada	85.06
USA	84.72
Czech Republic	84.67
Hungary	84.60
Italy	84.48

Bottom four countries and score

Country	Score
Niger	37.48
Madagascar	37.1
Eritrea	36.73
Somalia	27.66

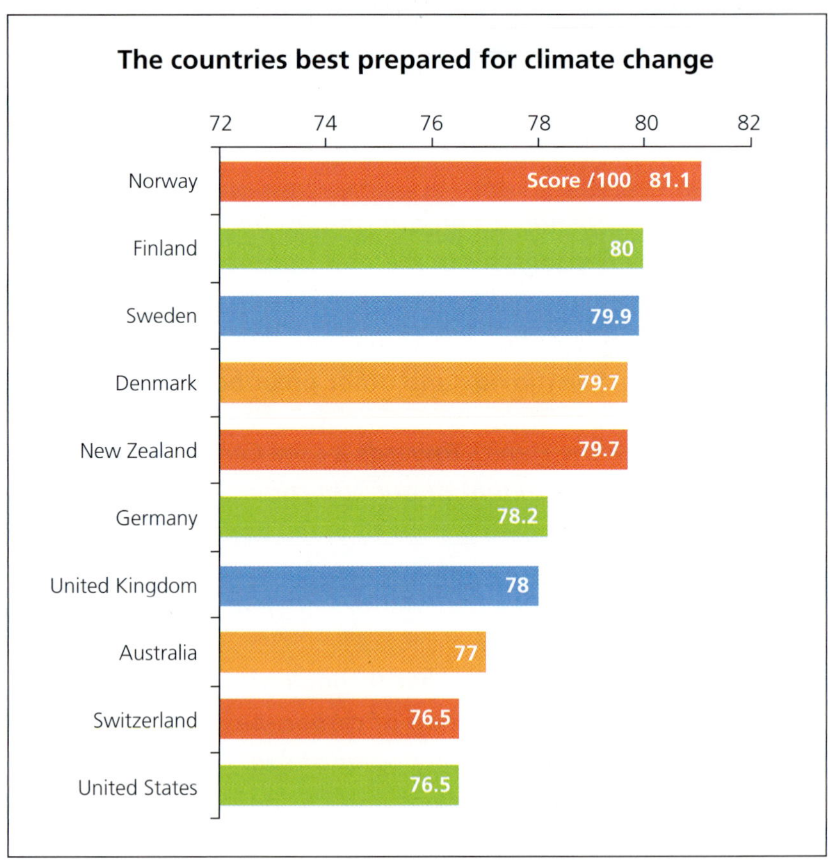

The World Economic Forum's Global Risks Report identifies the biggest global risks. The top risks always include environmental ones such as failure to adapt to climate change. This graph shows the results of a recent study measuring how well a country is adapting to climate change.

ISBN: 9780170418409

The top 10 in the 2017 Best Countries rankings of countries that cared most about the environment were, in order, Sweden, Norway, Finland, Switzerland, New Zealand, Denmark, Netherlands, Australia, Canada, and Germany.

Why Sweden ranked first

- Its official website says that for most of its people, sustainability is a way of life.
- More than half its energy came from renewables.
- Its people were top consumers in the EU of organic foods.
- It invested in green technology and eco-friendly public transportation.
- It had a growing number of 'passive houses' heated by body warmth, electrical appliances, lighting and sunlight.
- It had high ambitions and high solidarity with other countries.
- Its focus was not on what it has done but on what it still had to do.
- It wanted to have a vehicle fleet completely free of fossil fuels by 2030.
- It wanted to have no net greenhouse gas emissions by 2050.

By comparison, Somalia was still ranking around the bottom of such international surveys

- It had had many years of civil war.
- Biodiversity had taken a beating.
- It had no coastguard to stop fishing fleets from around the world illegally taking its seafood, damaging marine habitat, and running down stocks.
- Although the Somali Government, in partnership with the United Nations, had launched a campaign to encourage people to protect forests, people were still cutting down trees to produce charcoal for cooking and heating which released pollutants.
- Many people lacked access to clean water and safe sanitation.

SKILLS PRACTICE

1 Thinking precisely

Refer to the graph of the countries best prepared for climate change (page 62).

- **a** State how the names on it compare with the names which in a later ranking cared most about the environment.
- **b** State whether you think being prepared for climate change automatically means acting to stop it. Give a reason for your response.

2 Drawing a conclusion (deciding what you believe after considering facts)

Refer to the Environmental Performance Index (page 62).

- **a** Make a comment about how New Zealand did.
- **b** State reasons why you would expect New Zealand to do better than Somalia.

3 Looking at impact

- **a** State exactly what the data is about.
- **b** State how such data would impact on the Environmental Performance Index.

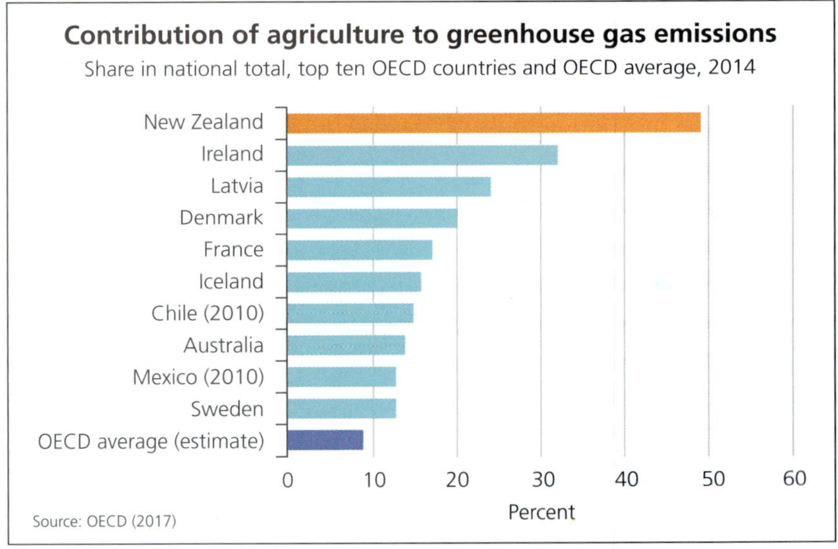

4 Thinking about attitude (way of feeling or thinking about something)

Refer to the image.

- **a** Locate the image in either a developed country or a developing country and give a reason for your location.
- **b** Describe the attitude shown in the image.
- **c** Give a reason why it is important to involve all generations in the environmental fight-back.

5 Understanding key performance indicators

A key performance indicator is something that can be measured to show how well things are going towards reaching a target, such as energy consumption. Make a list of possible environmental key performance indicators.

ISBN: 9780170418409

Fixing the hole above

World Ozone Day is 16 September to mark the signing of the Montreal Protocol on that date. The Montreal Protocol was an international treaty designed to protect the ozone layer by phasing out the making of many substances that caused the ozone to grow a 'hole'.

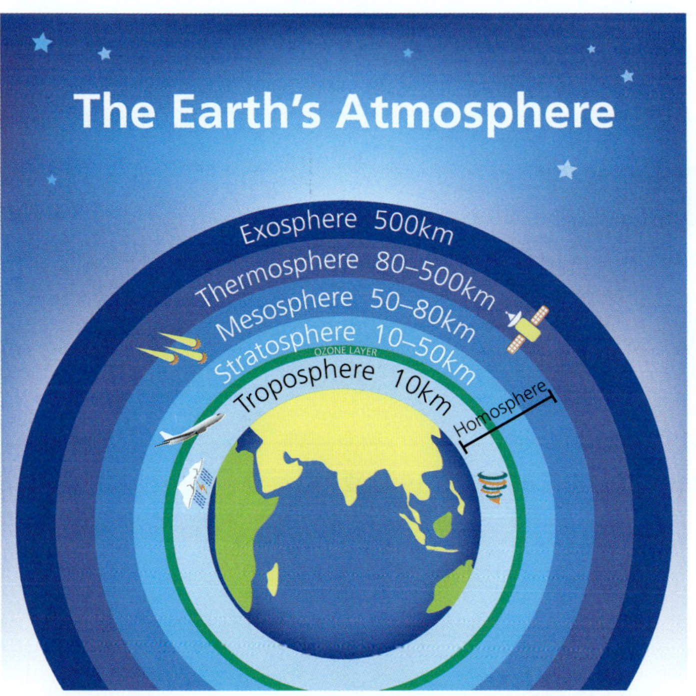

- Earth's atmosphere is the layer of gases called air that surrounds it.
- One layer is called the stratosphere and it contains a thin layer of ozone.
- The ozone layer filters out the sun's harmful ultraviolet radiation rays and so protects people and environment.
- The so-called hole described the way the ozone layer was getting thinner. This is called depletion.

The 'hole' formed over Antarctica each spring. It formed mainly there because of the extreme cold and large amount of light. Humans caused this to happen by using chemicals such as CFCs — chlorofluorocarbons — containing atoms of chlorine, carbon and fluorine, which had been put in aerosol spray cans and refrigerants. They went into the atmosphere and caused the ozone to break down.

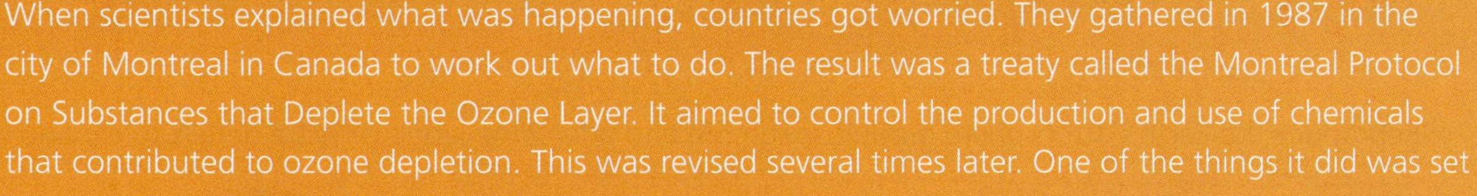

When scientists explained what was happening, countries got worried. They gathered in 1987 in the city of Montreal in Canada to work out what to do. The result was a treaty called the Montreal Protocol on Substances that Deplete the Ozone Layer. It aimed to control the production and use of chemicals that contributed to ozone depletion. This was revised several times later. One of the things it did was set out a phase-out time of 1996 for the use and production of CFCs in developed countries and 2010 in developing countries.

ISBN: 9780170418409

Results of the treaty

The treaty got 197 signatories, including New Zealand.

It was the first treaty in the history of the United Nations to get signed by all the members.

Scientists said in 2015 that the hole was around four million square kilometres smaller than it was in 2000. That was an area roughly the size of India.

Most scientists today say the ozone layer will eventually recover although maybe not until about 2050 or 2060. This is because even though the production of CFCs has stopped, there is still a lot of chlorine left in the atmosphere and it has a long lifetime before it decays.

Scientists say the ozone story is a role model for how to tackle global environmental problems, with countries working together to deal to a common threat.

SKILLS PRACTICE

1 Preparing an explanatory note

Write a short explanation to go under this graph. Include an explanation of what CFCs were, what happened to their production, and why.

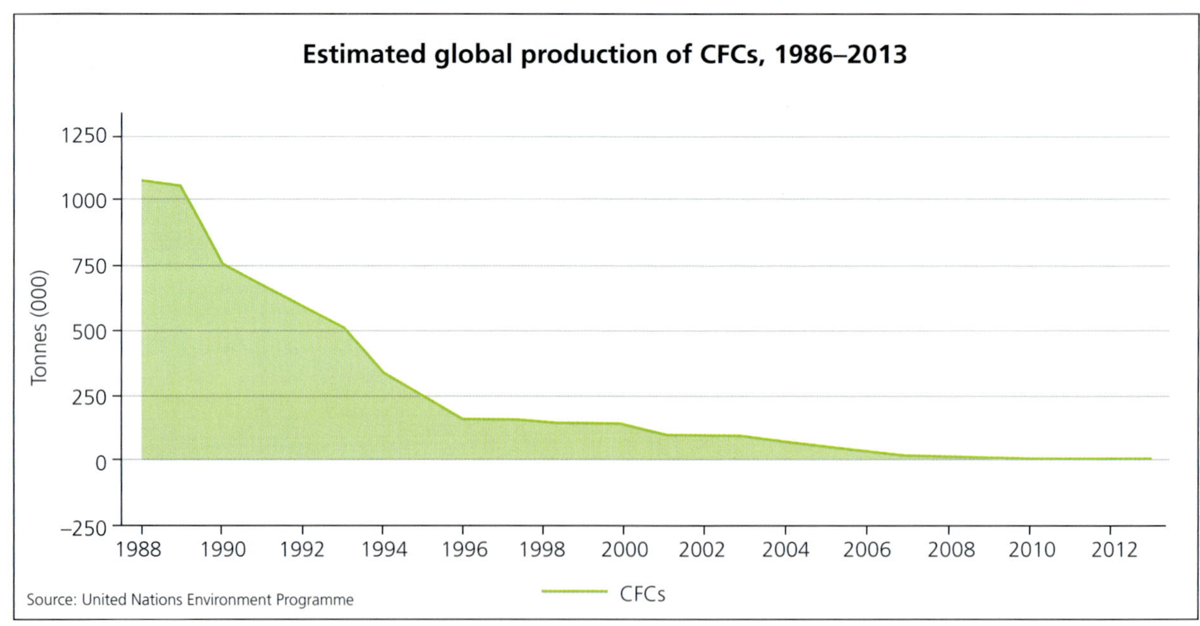

2 Reproducing

Reproduce the Earth's atmosphere graphic (page 65) and add some labels or extra details to expand it.

3 Equating action with image

State why trying to fix the ozone hole is an example of international cooperative action.

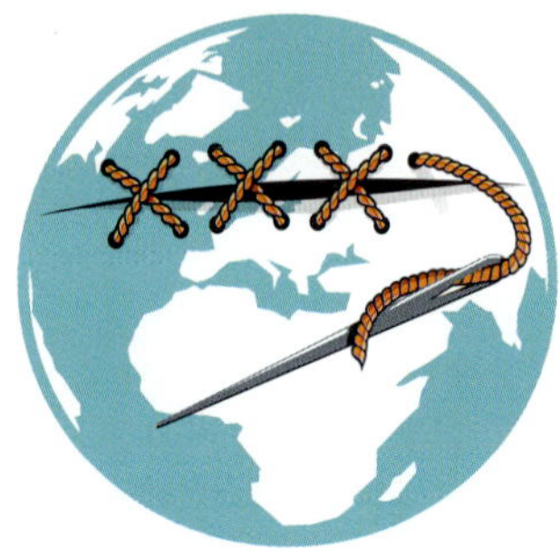

ISBN: 9780170418409

4 Finding meanings

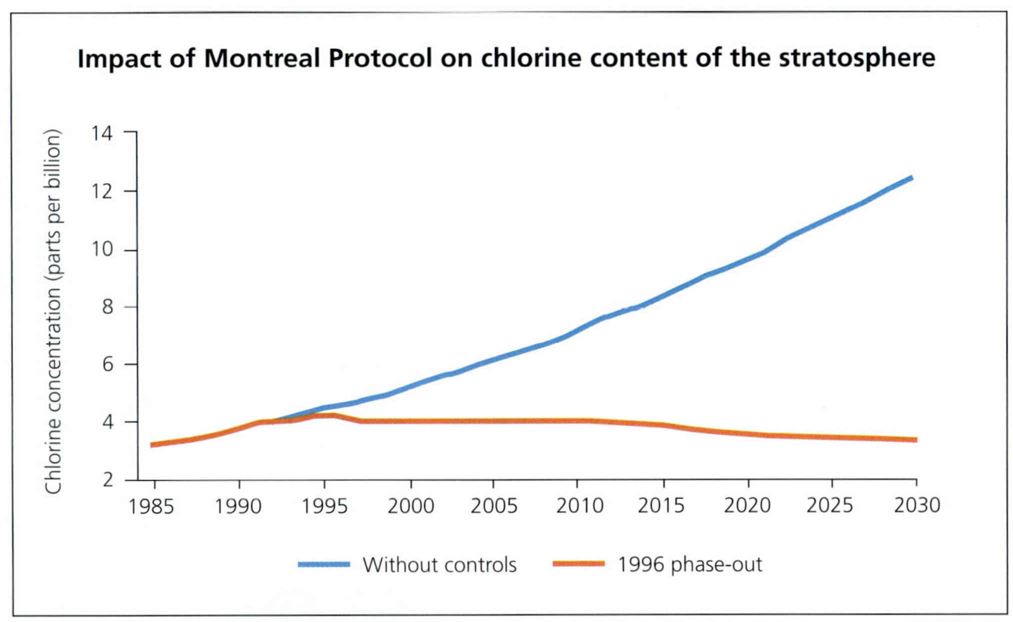

a Explain the meaning of Montreal, Protocol, chlorine, stratosphere, without controls, phase-out.

b Explain how your meanings show what the graph is about.

5 Grading

Give a grade out of 10 for this effort to describe the issue of the ozone hole. Explain your grading.

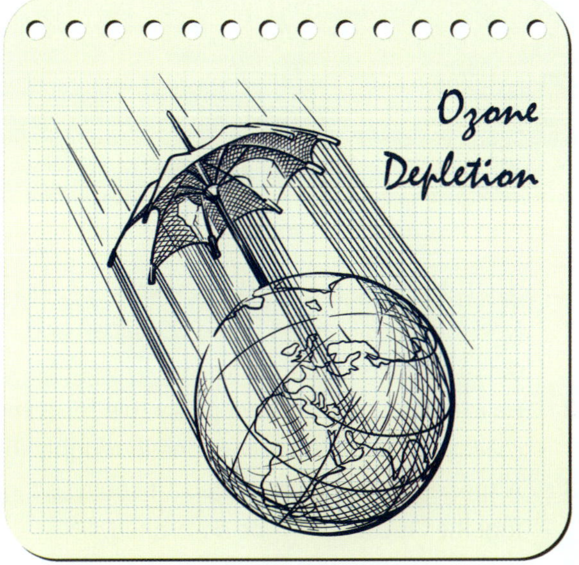

De-orbiting the junk

Space junk is the man-made stuff in orbit about Earth that no longer serves a useful function or has been created by accident such as a collision between a dead satellite and an operational satellite.

NASA says space junk won't go away unless humans force it to. Even if countries stopped launching into space today, the junk would stay.

Countries are trying to work together. There is a Space Debris Office at the European Space Agency looking for solutions. In May 2017 scientists from around the world came to Canberra's Space Environment Research Centre to brainstorm solutions. Private companies are working on cutting-edge solutions.

It might be as big as a spacecraft, or as small as a fleck of paint. It travels at speeds fast enough to damage a satellite or a spacecraft. Paint flecks, for example, have done so much damage that space shuttle windows have had to be replaced. Junk could make some orbits around Earth unusable.

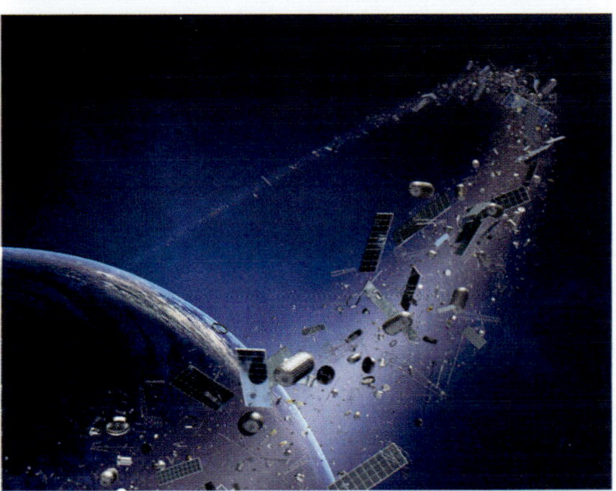

Examples of suggested solutions

1. New launches licensed in the US, Japan and Europe are now required to have a plan for getting satellites down at the end of their lives.
2. Have a one-up, one-down policy rule for companies. For every spacecraft a company launches, it must collect and de-orbit another one in roughly the same orbit.
3. A special junk removal spacecraft could use ion engines to track and dock with junk, collecting pieces together. It could then be de-orbited.
4. A space laser system could target and fire on junk as it goes by. It would vaporise small pieces and slow larger ones, lowering their orbit.
5. Lasers could push junk to make it fall back to Earth and burn up harmlessly in the atmosphere.
6. Creating electrodynamic drag with a tether hundreds of metres long could slow down junk, so it could burn up in the atmosphere.
7. Other kinds of capture mechanisms could be nets, harpoons, robotic arms and tentacles.
8. A space sweeper could capture junk, swing it towards Earth's atmosphere, and then swing on to the next junk.
9. A network of nanosatellites, connected with electrically conducting tape about three kilometres long, could knock junk down as it passes through Earth's magnetic field and produces voltage.
10. Satellites the size of football fields could orbit Earth and capture junk.
11. Dead satellites could be refurbished and recycled by robots that tag along on satellite launches.
12. A ground-based laser combined with a ground-based telescope could nudge junk out of the way and reduce the risk of collisions.

ISBN: 9780170418409

SKILLS PRACTICE 

1 Using a definition

Explain if, and why or why not, this man-made creation is space junk or not.

2 Understanding combinations

State how the cartoonist has combined two environmental issues in the one cartoon.

3 Making notes

Make notes about the following that you could contribute to a discussion.

Some people say a more urgent space environmental issue than space junk is space tourism, which could make global warming worse. Others say why worry about the space environment at all when the environment closer to home needs all the help it can get to fight back.

4 Considering ifs

a If you were in charge of advertising space flights, would you mention possible dangers of space junk? Why or why not?

b If you were using this image in a presentation about space junk, what would you say about the astronaut's rights and responsibilities? For example, a caption could be 'Enjoy your float but don't drop any tools.'

5 Thinking of viability (if capable of working effectively)

State what you think of the suggested solutions and if you think any sound more viable than others.

ISBN: 9780170418409

How you clean an ocean

Causes of ocean pollution

The first step to cleaning up a dirty environment is to admit it is dirty.

Bad news

Our Marine Environment 2016, the first report from the Ministry for the Environment and Statistics New Zealand about the marine environment, said New Zealand's oceans, coasts and marine wildlife were under growing pressure.

Global greenhouse gas emissions were causing ocean acidification and warming was causing sea-level crisis.

Most native marine birds and many mammals were threatened with or at risk of extinction.

Coasts were the most degraded of all marine areas, due to sediment and nutrients washed off the land, introduced marine pests, and seabed trawling and dredging.

But also good news

Where New Zealand had identified the issues and worked to fix them, results were happening. For example, changes in fishing practices had almost halved the number of seabirds caught.

Solutions from around the world

- The most low-tech way to protect the oceans from further trash is to persuade people to stop putting it into the ocean.
- Many cities are installing booms in rivers and estuaries to capture plastic trash before it washes into the sea.

  ISBN: 9780170418409

- Fishing for Energy in the USA helps fishermen properly dispose of old gear at no cost. Some fishermen get others' lost gear out of the ocean. Metal parts are recycled, and everything else is converted into electricity. About a ton of old nets produce enough electricity to power a house for 25 days.
- Plastic Bank company created a blockchain digital currency and exchange platform to encourage people to collect plastic before it hits the ocean, and bring it to a recycling centre where it is pelletised, maybe for 3D printers to turn into packaging. In exchange people can get cash, Wi-Fi access or electricity to charge mobiles.
- Global Ghost Gear Initiative supports projects around the world that capture and make use of abandoned gear, such as converting it into carpet tiles.
- A teenager set up The Ocean Cleanup Company, which had a plan to clear out trash with a drifting V-shaped system. It announced it would start clearing out the Great Pacific Garbage Patch in 2018.
- The Seawer Skyscraper is a massive portable, self-supported solar-hydro power station that generates electricity using seawater while removing plastic waste. Purified seawater is released back into the ocean.
- The SeaVax is a solar- and wind-powered, self-driving ship with special sensors to detect the plastic it then sucks up and sonar technology that protects marine life.
- Seabin is an automated rubbish bin built from recycled materials that is fixed to a dock with a water pump creating flow to suck floating rubbish into a natural fibre bag and then pumping the water back out.
- The Waste Shark, an aquatic drone about the size of a car, vacuums up floating trash.

Linked to cleaning the ocean are efforts to save coral reefs

- NASA has developed instruments such as the Portable Remote Imaging Spectrometer to study coral reefs from an airplane.
- Rescue a Reef programme in Florida's Key Biscayne has scientists who are certified divers replanting parts of the reef with the help of citizen scientists who are members of the community. They first collect recently grown coral from 'trees' installed in the water and then secure it to the ocean floor.
- The small village of Cabo Pulmo in Mexico acted to get a protected area around its reef to let reef and fish stocks recover. It got support from international scientists and lobbied the government. Excellent results after 10 years of protection proved to the world that ocean management led by locals does work.

Cabo Pulmo in Mexico.

Florida's Key Biscayne.

ISBN: 9780170418409

SKILLS PRACTICE

1 Revising

Revise your knowledge of the spelling and location of the world's oceans.

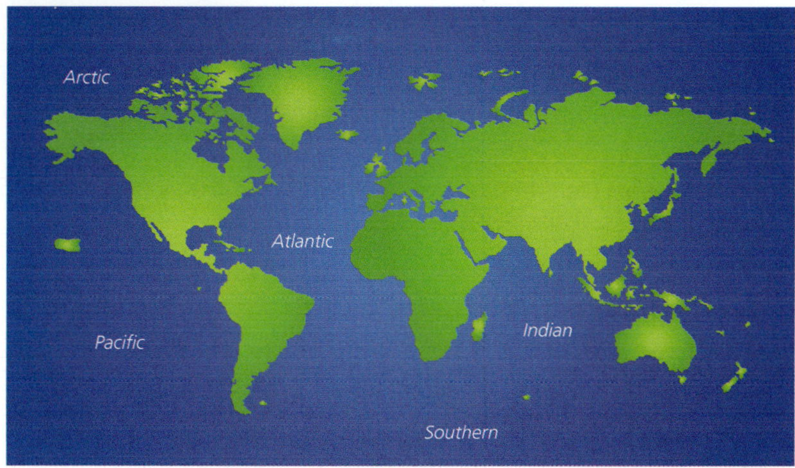

2 Sensing hope

Read the following and state how each one offers hope for helping oceans.

1. Oceans offer opportunities for renewable energy technologies, such as offshore wind farms, tidal or wave energy devices.
2. Solving ocean pollution often starts with groups of people and that can develop into getting government support.
3. Some entrepreneurs of companies to clean oceans say their mission will only truly be over when the company is out of business.
4. Cleaning up the Great Pacific Garbage Patch using conventional methods would take thousands of years and tens of billions of dollars but many people see that as a challenge for future technologies.
5. Research shows 80 percent of pollution in the marine environment comes from the land.
6. NASA's Jet Propulsion Laboratory conducted a study to find how much of the excess water from rising sea levels continents absorb. Two orbiting satellites showed that the continents slow the rise of sea levels by nearly 20 percent every year.

3 Being specific

State which specific aspect to do with the ocean the cartoon addresses and how it addresses it.

4 Assessing fairness

Read the following comment and state whether or not you think it is a fair thing to say as far as environmental issues to do with oceans are concerned. Give your reasoning.

'The greatest threat to our planet is the belief that someone else will save it.'* *(Robert Swan)

Now what's this I hear about rising oceans?

5 Deciding priority (most important)

Many ideas to clean up oceans and to address rising sea levels need funding to get off the ground. State, as an investor, which of the two issues you would be most interested in looking at and why.

ISBN: 9780170418409

Plastic bags are so back in the day

28

The *bad* news

Henderson Island, part of the Pitcairns, is a UNESCO world heritage site in the south Pacific Ocean, about halfway between New Zealand and Chile. Nobody lives on it, yet when researchers went there in 2017, they found an estimated 38 million pieces of garbage washed up on the beaches. Most of it was plastic, things like toy soldiers, dominoes, toothbrushes and hardhats, and its density was the highest recorded anywhere in the world. At the same time, research predicted that unless the world acted, by 2050 there will be more plastic in the world's oceans by weight than fish.

Plastic in rivers.

Global plastic pollution crisis

Plastic on beaches.

Plastic in the ocean.

Plastic in dump sites.

Plastic up in the mountains.

The *good* news

More and more people around the world are protesting against plastic pollution. A campaign to break free from plastic began in July 2016 when people from all around the world met in the Philippines and pledged to join a BreakFreeFromPlastic movement. 'We believe in a world where the land, sky, oceans and water is home to an abundance of life, not an abundance of plastic, and where the air we breathe, the water we drink and the food we eat is free of toxic by-products of plastic pollution,' it said. 'In this world the principles of environmental justice, social justice, public health and human rights lead government policy, not the demands of elites and corporations.'

Over a hundred environmental organisations signed up to the BreakFreeFromPlastic movement. One was the Surfrider Foundation, which has run many campaigns against plastic.

Examples of new anti-plastic technology

1 A machine the size of a tennis court in a trash processing centre near London breaks down plastic products and turns them into usable materials or energy-producing oil.

2 Scientists recently announced this creature, the waxworm, could solve or help solve the plastic crisis. It is a tiny caterpillar larva of the wax moth and it often lives in beehives where it chomps through beeswax. The scientists had found the waxworms could eat through polyethylene, the most common plastic in the world, which is mainly used for plastic bags and packaging and is hard to break down. They thought this finding could be engineered into an environmentally friendly solution on an industrial scale and the enzymes could be sprayed directly on to landfills or infused into water plants to break down plastic in the environment.

SKILLS PRACTICE

1 Understanding pledging

Refer to the BreakFreeFromPlastic pledge.

a State what a pledge is.

b State what are the three main differences to the world the movement wants.

2 Running a competition

The first commercially successful plastic arrived in 1907. A hundred years later some people were working to alert the planet about the damage plastic causes and to realise that efforts to biodegrade plastic had to come alongside efforts to prevent the use of it in the first place.

Describe how you would run a competition to see who can come up with the most suggestions of how an individual can cut down on the use of plastic.

ISBN: 9780170418409

3 Combining elements

Explain how you would combine these four elements to make a poster for an anti-plastic awareness campaign.

> ***'The leatherback turtle can keep itself warm in cold water, dive over 1000 meters below sea level, travel thousands of miles and gulp down a Portuguese man-of-war but is threatened by the inert plastic shopping bag.'***
> ***(N. Mrosovky)***

> ***The brown paper bag, which the plastic bag practically displaced, has a biodegradable period of about a month.***

4 Rearranging for sense

Rearrange the following sentences about the waxworm discovery into an order that makes sense.

Were the creatures just chewing up the plastic or were they breaking it down chemically?

Soon she saw the waxworms were crawling around her place and the plastic bag was full of holes.

They are made of a plastic called polyethylene that can take decades to break down.

The plastic degraded.

Scientist and beekeeper Federica Bertocchini, who worked at the Institute of Biomedicine and Biotechnology of Cantabria in Spain, found waxworms had infested her beehives.

The researchers found the worms transformed the plastic into ethylene glycol, which is commonly used in antifreeze.

Humans use over a trillion plastic bags every year.

This showed it was something chemical.

She and a team of researchers tested by grinding some waxworms into a pulp and spreading it on the polyethylene plastic.

She put the worm-infested parts in a plastic bag.

5 Follow-up

Find out if anything came of the discovery that waxworms ate plastic.

Attacking river muggers

Million litres of fresh water available per person per year

Canada 82, Australia 22, USA 9, China 2, UK 2, New Zealand 145

New Zealand is lucky to have so many rivers.

Conflict over use of New Zealand's fresh water

Industry.

Tourism.

Agriculture.

Locals.

Energy.

A 2016 video from Greenpeace said that over 60 percent of monitored rivers in New Zealand were unsafe to swim in. It highlighted the contribution of dairy farming to river pollution.

Examples of river muggers

- Fertiliser runoff.
- Animal faeces and urine.
- Land clearance and building causing silt build-up.
- Broken sewers letting sewage into stormwater systems.
- Getting rid of the trees and wetlands that stop rain putting sediment in.
- Industry discharging waste water.
- Human waste in areas without toilets.
- Water runoff from roads.
- Erosion of hills and banks.

ISBN: 9780170418409

Examples of muggers' attackers

DairyNZ, an organisation funded by New Zealand's 10,000 dairy farmers, brought in a plan to protect waterways on farmland. It said its farmers had spent over a billion dollars protecting waterways from pollution. Examples of efforts included fencing off rivers from livestock, building high-tech effluent systems including ones that farmers can control by phone when away, riparian planting (riparian = to do with banks of a river), which means planting trees along the banks, feeding cows different types of feed to reduce nitrogen in urine, and trying different types of grasses that can better absorb nitrogen before it seeps into the soil.

The government's Clean Water package included a target that 90 percent of New Zealand rivers and lakes be swimmable by 2040, and details of proposals to exclude stock from waterways by 2030. It also launched the $100 million Freshwater Improvement Fund.

The fund committed $100 million over 10 years to help communities improve the management of fresh water.

The Lake Brunner Project got funding to help deal with the decline in its water quality by making buffer strips of fencing and planting along streams to reduce pollutants entering the lake, and the development of environmental farm plans for farmers to help them reduce nutrient runoff.

Canterbury got known as the irrigation capital of New Zealand because its dairying needed so much water, and the Canterbury Water Management Strategy, which tells farmers the amount of pollution their animals are allowed to produce, had demanded they reduce nitrate leaching into groundwater by 36 percent by 2035. A plan from 2017 hoped half this reduction would come through aquifer recharging, which involved placing filtered water from an irrigation scheme in a large pond, drilling holes and getting the water to seep down into underground aquifers.

aquifer = an underground layer of something like rock that contains water or lets water pass through it

SKILLS PRACTICE 

1 **Arguing a case** (giving evidence for your ideas)
Make a case for the setting of the cartoon being located in a specific part of New Zealand.

2 **Making a visual**
A point source of pollution comes from an identifiable single source, such as a pipe into a river. A diffuse source is where the pollution has no specific point of discharge.

Make a visual to show the difference.

3 Close reading

Study the following and answer the questions about it.

Land, Air, Water Aotearoa (LAWA) is a website set up by like-minded organisations to give information for over 1100 freshwater sites. It wants to help local communities find the balance between using natural resources and maintaining water quality and availability. It is a partnership between 16 regional councils, Cawthron Institute, Ministry for the Environment and Massey University, and has been supported by the Tindall Foundation.

- **a** How does LAWA get its name?
- **b** What does 'like-minded' mean?
- **c** Elaborate on the balance it wants to help local communities find.
- **d** Which partner is most likely to be New Zealand's largest independent science organisation specialising in science that looks after the environment?
- **e** Suggest a time when you might use LAWA.

4 Commenting on a cartoon

- **a** Comment on whether or not the cartoon does any of the following.
  - **i** Identifies an issue.
  - **ii** Indicates a culprit.
  - **iii** Suggests solutions.
  - **iv** Gives cause for hope.
- **b** Comment on how you could alter the cartoon to show a more up-to-date approach.

5 Looking at an image

Hurunui River in Canterbury.

- **a** State why there might be cause for concern about the river.
- **b** State why there is no magical silver bullet that will instantly clean all rivers.

ISBN: 9780170418409

Jean Batten would be amazed

When Kiwi Jean Batten was making her record-breaking solo flights across the world in the 1930s, nobody talked about the impact of her plane's fuel on the environment. If she was flying today, she would be amazed. Not only at the change in planes but also at the talk of aviation fuel. She would learn that if the aviation sector was a country, it would be the eighth-largest emitter of greenhouse gases in the world — using planes and helicopters to move people and cargo around the world produces around 2 percent of the world's planet-warming gases. This is why scientists are looking for ways to keep planes in the air without further damaging the air.

Jean Batten.

International Civil Aviation Organization (ICAO) has said it will cap net carbon emissions from international aviation at 2020 levels with measures such as biofuels.

Biofuels have been shown to reduce the carbon footprint of aviation fuel by up to 80 percent over their full life cycle. Scientists say if commercial aviation were to get just 6 percent of its fuel from biofuel by 2020, this would reduce its overall carbon footprint by 5 percent.

While solar, electric and hydrogen-propelled aircraft are being researched, it is not expected they will be usable in the near or medium future.

Traditional aviation fuel = non-renewable fossil fuel designed for use in planes.

Aviation biofuel = renewable fuel made from sustainable sources such as vegetable oils, sugars and algae, designed for use in planes.

Fuels like methanol and ethanol are not practical for aviation because they have very low energy densities, which means they don't have enough punch.

Biofuels need to be sustainable, which means they do not compete with food supplies, and do not consume too much agricultural land or fresh water.

ISBN: 9780170418409

In 2008, Virgin Airlines became the first airline to fly a commercial airliner with biofuel oil in one of the four main fuel tanks.

Later that year New Zealand flew a Boeing 747 with a 50/50 mix of biofuel and conventional jet fuel for two hours.

Since then there have been several thousand commercial flights on biofuels, and airlines and their partners around the world are starting to make this a normal part of airline energy planning.

Projects are working on getting biofuels up and running. For example, LanzaTech is in partnership with Virgin Atlantic. The company was founded in New Zealand, is now based in the US, has a production facility in China, and gets jet fuel from waste industrial gases from steel mills, using a fermentation process.

A symposium (meeting) on sustainable aviation was held in 2017 in Kiev, Ukraine, to address aviation issues such as encouraging the use of biofuels.

Many airports are going green. If you were flying into this airport you would be at Boston Logan, which got the first LEED certificate (Leadership in Energy and Environmental Design) in the USA. It has wind turbines and solar panels, an asphalt mix that reduced CO_2 emissions and saved fuel and energy during construction, compressed natural gas (CNG) fuelling stations and charging stations for electric vehicles at the airport, Clean Air Cabs and a Clean Vehicle Preferred Parking programme.

SKILLS PRACTICE

1 Key understandings

Complete the following sentences so you end up with key understandings of the topic.

- **a** Traditional aviation fuel impacts on the environment by …
- **b** To be sustainable, biofuels need to be …
- **c** Electric, solar and hydrogen-powered planes are …
- **d** Biofuels can reduce the carbon footprint of aviation fuel by …
- **e** By 2020, any increase in airline CO_2 emissions will need to be …
- **f** If commercial aviation got just 6 percent of its fuel from biofuel by 2020, it would reduce …

2 Who/what am I?

- **a** I am the capital city of Ukraine and I hosted a symposium on sustainable aviation.
- **b** I am non-renewable fuel designed for use in planes.
- **c** I am renewable fuel designed for use in planes.
- **d** I was the first airline to fly a commercial airliner with biofuel.
- **e** I was the first airport to get a LEED certificate.
- **f** I am the plane New Zealand flew with its first biofuel.
- **g** I am a Kiwi-founded company working on aviation biofuel.
- **h** I am known as ICAO.

ISBN: 9780170418409

3 Formulating questions

Formulate five questions about this topic such as, Are there really green aeroplanes?

4 Understanding a complex diagram

Aviation became the first sector in the world to get a uniform approach to addressing climate change when delegates to an ICAO assembly agreed to it. This diagram is one thing aviation used to describe its approach.

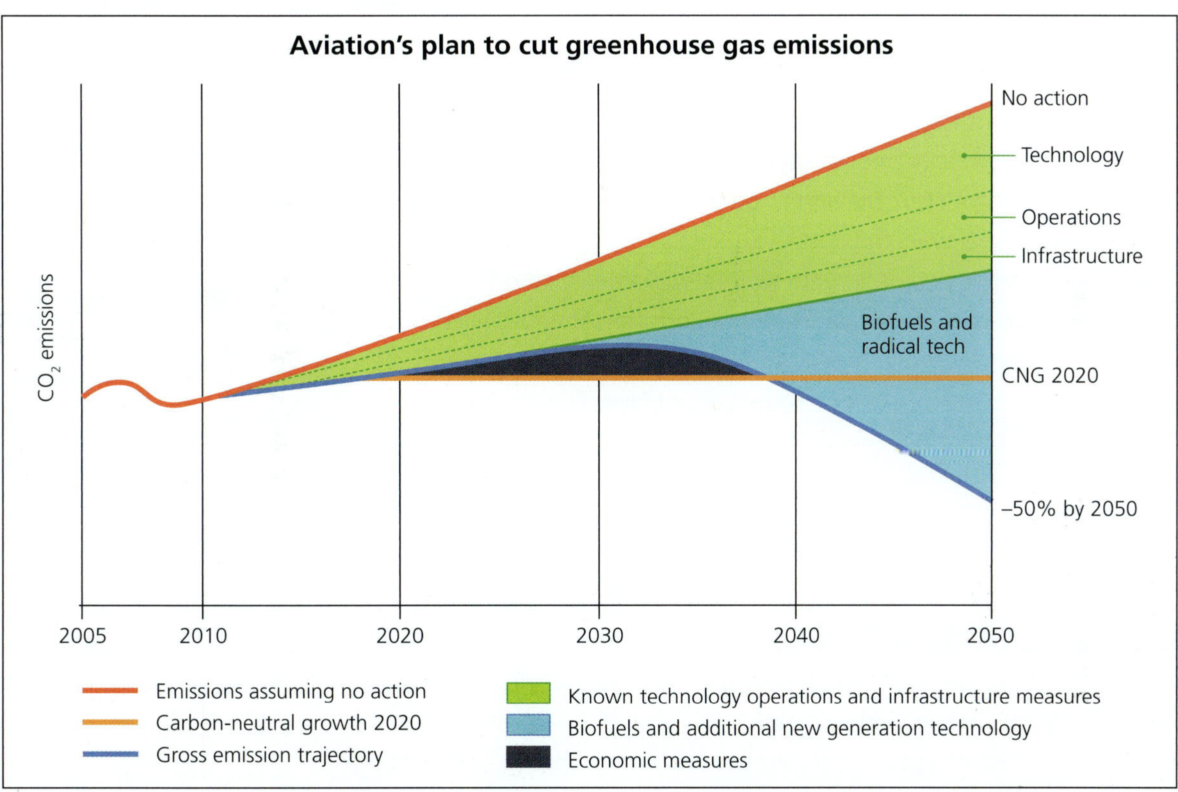

There is a lot of information on the diagram, which makes it complex.
List as many points about it as you can that would help explain it to somebody else.

5 Detective work

Yield of various plant oils in litres per hectare per year

Corn	227
Soybeans	447
Safflower	780
Sunflower	950
Castor	1412
Coconut	2290
Palm	5951
X	99999

X can be used to make aviation biofuel. It grows quickly, consumes carbon dioxide and releases oxygen as it grows, does not compete with agriculture, can purify waste water as it grows, and it stores energy in the form of oil better than other natural or engineered processes.

Work out what X is.

A DOC for the environment

- New Zealand is a democracy, which means people have the right to choose who governs them. They do this by electing members of Parliament to represent them.
- As many people put the environment at or near the top of the list of issues that most concern them, no government can afford to ignore environmental issues.

- DOC (Department of Conservation) is the government agency in charge of looking after New Zealand's diversity of plants and animals that make up the natural heritage.
- Its vision is for New Zealand to be the greatest living space on Earth: Kaore he wahi i tua atu i a Aotearoa, hei wahi noho i te ao.
- It encourages people to get involved with conservation.
- It helps conservation gain from more business partnerships.
- It manages Crown land set aside for conservation and protection, which is about 30 percent of New Zealand's land area or about 8 million hectares.

conservation = protecting something and making sure it survives

Results of a recent DOC survey of the attitudes of Kiwis to it and to conservation

- Most felt that the most threatening species to native plants, birds, animals or natural environments were possums, rats, stoats and wild cats.
- Methods most acceptable for pest control were trapping and hunting.
- Methods of pest control most felt uncomfortable about were poison bait and herbicides dropped by aircraft.
- Most believed connection with nature improved their lives.
- Personal benefits of conservation were protecting the natural environment for children and protecting plants and animals.
- Most rated conservation as being important to them.
- Over half in the past 12 months had engaged in at least one conservation action such as donating money to a cause, getting information about a conservation issue, helping to raise awareness about conservation issues, and expressing opinions about issues through online forums.
- Most had a favourable view of DOC.
- Key reasons for unfavourable views were pest control and 1080 poison.

Controversial issue — use of 1080 poison

In March 2015, Fonterra and Federated Farmers got anonymous blackmail threats warning that if the use of 1080 was not stopped by the end of that month, infant formula in supermarkets would be poisoned. Police charged a man and he was sentenced to eight and a half years in prison.

ISBN: 9780170418409

For 1080

- Suited for use as there are no native ground-living mammals to harm.
- Best way to control pests over large and inaccessible areas.
- Biodegradable so breaks down naturally and does not leave residues in water, soil, plants or animals or build up in the food chain.
- Use is strictly regulated and monitored.
- Pests are there 365 days of every year; 1080 might get used one day every three years.

Against 1080

- Toxic to all birds.
- No proper scientific evidence that it helps native species survive.
- Alternative methods of pest control are not explored or used.
- Can be wind-blown or washed downhill.
- Can travel down into the soil and ground water.
- Kills non-target species, including dogs.

SKILLS PRACTICE

1 Evaluating a logo

The logo is based on the story of Maori creation. Blue is Ranginui, the Sky Father, and green is Papatuanuku, the Earth Mother. The white koru is new life, strength and a continuing journey, and the shield shows protection and care.

a State what you think makes a good logo.

b State your response to the DOC logo.

2 Differentiating

a State which type New Zealand has.

b State if you think any one type is more likely than others to set up a DOC and why that is so.

Types of government

3 Making suggestions

Each year DOC runs a Conservation Week to encourage people to get involved in nature and help protect it. For example, in 2017 Conservation Week ran from 14-22 October and DOC encouraged people to show their backyards some love by getting involved in protecting, growing, and caring for nature.

a Suggest a suitable definition for conservation.

b Suggest reasons why there was no such thing as Conservation Week until 1969.

c Suggest reasons why the week is getting more popular and well-known.

d Suggest three activities people might have done for 2017's Conservation Week. Built a Weta Hotel or a Lizard Lounge? Planted heirloom vegetables?

4 Debating

Prepare ideas for a debate about the use of 1080.

5 Supplying information

The cartoon refers to a faulty temperature control that killed about 800 rare giant snails taken from the West Coast.

a Supply a location and a reaction to a DOC action.

b Supply a title.

ISBN: 9780170418409

Fighting the predators

One day about a hundred years ago, local school children got the day off to celebrate the release of Australian possums into the forest at Mt Bruce near Masterton. The possums were to form the basis of a fur industry in the Wairarapa. Mt Bruce is now a bird sanctuary, and millions of dollars have been spent freeing the area of possums.

DOC has set up Predator Free 2050, which aims to eradicate possums, rats and stoats by 2050. The idea is that predators have been wiped out on many islands, so why can't they be wiped out on the main islands? A bigger tool box is now available to get rid of pests, with new techniques such as traps that reset themselves, predator-specific toxins, and GPS-guided aerial application of 1080. Regional councils and OSPRI (Operational Solutions for Primary Industries) are investing in predator control. Groups are joining up to get predator-free communities, such as Predator Free Dunedin Memorandum of Understanding, which was signed by 19 signatories in 2017.

predator = an animal that hunts and kills other animals

Predator-proof fence.

Pest trap.

 ISBN: 9780170418409

New Zealand is a world leader in conservation technology and research. It has tens of thousands of volunteers and private landowners working on protecting habitats. An example of a fenced sanctuary is Project Janszoon in Abel Tasman National Park. It is a privately funded trust working with DOC, the Abel Tasman Birdsong Trust, the community and local iwi to restore the park. Launched in 2012, it will finish work in 2042 on the 100-year anniversary of the establishment of the park and the 400-year anniversary of Abel Tasman's sighting of Aotearoa.

Projects in Hawke's Bay

Cape Kidnappers is one of the biggest mainland gannet colonies in the world. It is located 15 kilometres east of Hastings in Hawke's Bay.

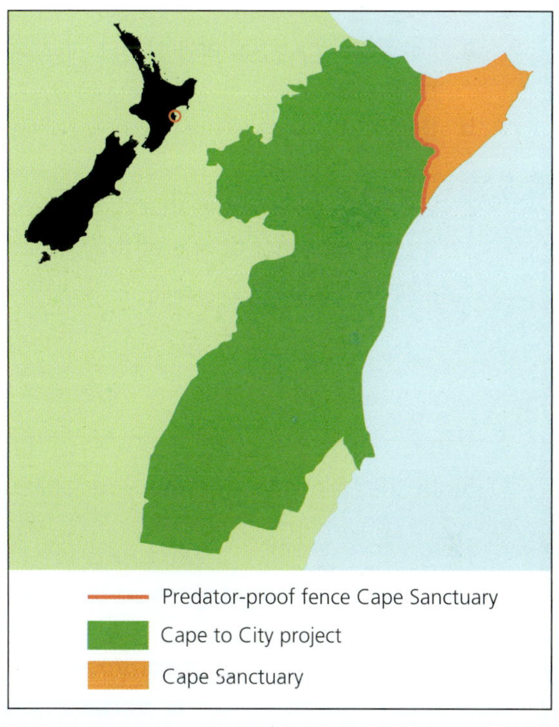

Cape Sanctuary:

- is a privately owned and funded restoration project with volunteers
- is located on three properties on the Cape Kidnappers peninsula
- aims to bring back the birds and other creatures it once had
- took almost a year to build a fence across the peninsula to stop predators.

Cape to City project:

- is jointly funded over 2015–20 by the Aotearoa Foundation, DOC, Hawke's Bay Regional Council, Landcare Research, Cape Sanctuary
- aims to restore habitats by projects such as planting native trees, bringing back native birds, and improving water quality.

SKILLS PRACTICE

1 Locating

- **a** Describe the general locations of Cape Sanctuary and Cape to City project.
- **b** Describe the locations of the two in relation to each other.

2 Managing a project

- **a** List skills any good project manager should have.
- **b** Decide if you have the necessary skills to manage a project.
- **c** List special challenges that might face a project manager of one of the Hawke's Bay projects.

3 Values

Study the following and state your opinions about any of the ideas in them.

Possums are classed as pests in New Zealand, as they threaten the survival of many native plants and birds.

DOC recommends humanely killing possums by shooting or poisoning them or hitting them on the head.

Many rural schools throughout the country hold possum hunts as fundraisers. One school was criticised for holding a best-dressed dead possum competition. Another school was criticised for drowning possums.

4 Naming places

- **a** List all the places with proper names (clue = spelled with capitals).
- **b** See how many origins of the names you can find.

5 Predicting public reaction

Getting to a predator-free New Zealand by 2050 will involve new technology, and also the public's agreement that it should be used. One idea put forward is gene technology to spread a particular characteristic, such as producing infertile offspring, through the population of predators. It could use a gene drive that would get the genetic sequence through the whole population so offspring will inherit the targeted gene rather than the usual 50 percent chance of inheriting a gene from each parent.

- **a** State how gene technology might be able to lead to the end of possums in New Zealand.
- **b** State if you think the public would all be in favour of using gene technology against predators, and why or why not.

  ISBN: 9780170418409

33

Nasties not needed

Biosecurity is

- keeping a country free of unwanted organisms (animals and plants)
- controlling, managing or eradicating them if they arrive.

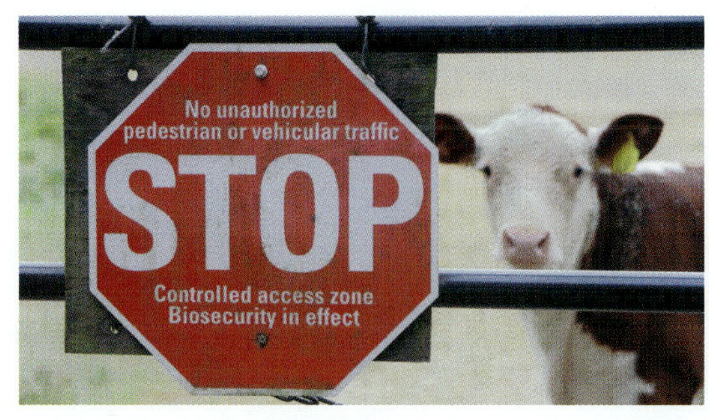

An example:

Venomous Australian redback spiders arrived in Otago in the 1980s probably with goods such as steel products.

The spiders now catch critically endangered chafer beetles.

The spiders invade the territory of endangered species of weta.

The spiders find homes in old rabbit holes.

If you find a redback spider, please report this to MPI Biosecurity.

MPI (Ministry for Primary Industries) is the lead agency for biosecurity In New Zealand, which was the first country in the world to pass a Biosecurity Act.

- It puts inspectors at entry points such as airports and ports.
- Passengers have to sign a form saying that they do not have anything that is a biosecurity risk.
- Inspectors use beagles to help check for unwanted organisms; they incinerate any nasties they find.
- MPI also runs a system of rapid response to findings of new, harmful pests and diseases.

ISBN: 9780170418409

GIA (Government Industry Agreement) works as a partnership between government and primary industry (industry that produces and mines raw materials such as farming and fishing) to deal with biosecurity threats.

Industry organisations that sign up to GIA share the decision-making, responsibilities and costs of preparing for and responding to biosecurity breaches (breaking through biosecurity and getting an unwanted organism into the country).

The GIA's idea is that industry and government will get better biosecurity by working together.

An example of how GIA works:

- MPI has a fruit-fly trapping programme that watches for 100 species of unwanted fruit flies, including Queensland fruit fly. It sets over seven thousand traps around the country. Any catch triggers a response.
- In February 2015, a small population of the Queensland fruit fly was found in the Auckland suburb of Grey Lynn.
- Kiwifruit Vine Health and Pipfruit NZ, which had signed up for GIA, worked alongside MPI to decide a response and give resources and support to their members.
- They set up a Controlled Area around where the fruit flies were found. For 1.5 kilometres in each direction, they cut down on the movement of fruit and vegetables, baited fruit trees to attract and kill fruit flies, and inspected fruit from local trees.
- When they had trapped no more Queensland fruit flies, they declared New Zealand fruit fly-free.

A lot of information goes out to the public to get help in fighting for biosecurity. When the invasive algae didymo, which people call rocksnot, was discovered in South Island rivers, the message went out to remind people to Check, Clean, Dry all boats and gear between waterways and report any didymo sightings to the MPI 0800 hotline.

ISBN: 9780170418409

SKILLS PRACTICE

1 Understanding a system

system = a set of things working together to carry out a specific action

Show how GIA is a system that helps the environment.

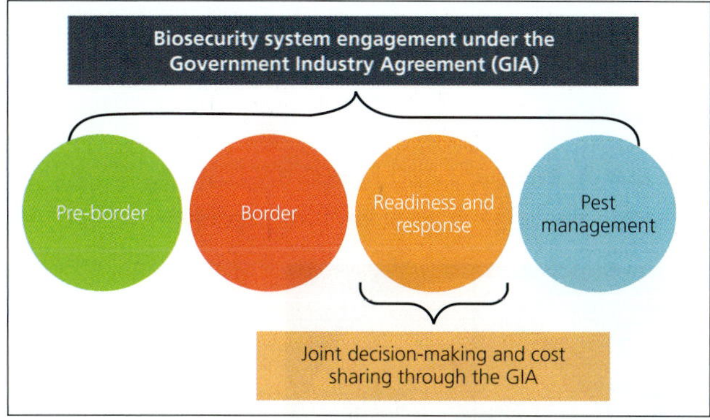

2 Cartoon dialogue

Study the cartoon about didymo (page 88) and explain how the cartoonist has used dialogue to do the following.

- **a** Include the nickname of didymo.
- **b** Show biosecurity is about internal as well as national border protection.
- **c** Stress the seriousness of the issue.

3 Research

Choose one of the following to find out how it may have got into New Zealand and what happened after it was found.

Painted apple moth **Varroa mite** **PSA** **Great white butterfly** **Myrtle rust**

4 Identifying

Identify the following in the cartoon.

- **a** The two people and how the cartoonist has showed who they are.
- **b** How the people are acting and why.

5 Modern language

A lot of detail and technical language like the following can be off-putting. See if you can rewrite it to make it easier to understand.

The New Zealand government has a Biosecurity 2025 direction statement. It includes a mission for biosecurity, principles to guide the way, directions to get the priority areas for action and improvement, targets for 2025, and actions for a starting point. Its directions include a biosecurity team of 4.7 million, so every Kiwi becomes a biosecurity risk manager and every business manages its own biosecurity risk, a tool box for tomorrow which uses science and technology to change the way New Zealand does biosecurity, smart and free-flowing information which taps into data and data analysis, and effective leadership and governance to support all parts of the system.

'Back off,' trumpet the elephants

I am an elephant and I need my tusks for weapons against attackers and to help me get food and water. Poachers want to kill me for my ivory tusks like they kill tens of thousands of other elephants every year.

I am an elephant tusk made of ivory. Humans have used me for centuries to make things such as handles for daggers, piano keys and works of art.

I am a baby elephant. I watched poachers kill my mother and people think that will make me attack humans later. But a ranger rescued me and now I live in an elephant orphanage, where I see many people are doing all they can to make sure elephants do not become extinct.

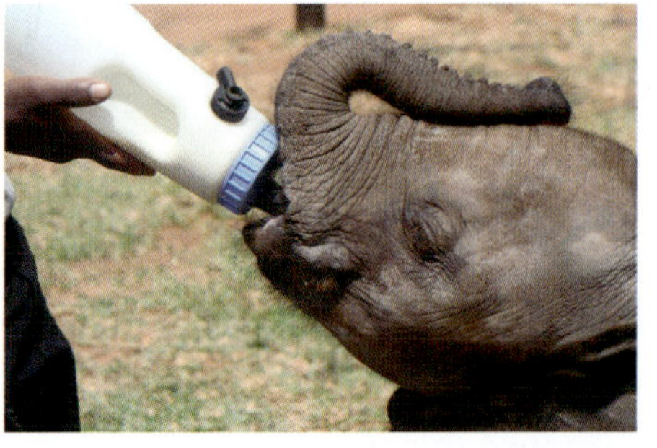

I am an ecotourist. I don't support sanctuaries that operate elephant rides or performances but I like to visit places that help keep elephants safe.

ISBN: 9780170418409

I am an ex-poacher. A warden who caught me poaching gave me a chance to become a game ranger and protect wildlife. Now I get a regular pay cheque, which is good for my family, and a uniform that shows I'm doing an important job. I want poachers to see that ivory brings in once-only cash but a living elephant keeps on earning money through ecotourism.

I am the famous Ivory Burning Site Monument in the Nairobi National Park, where Kenya has organised the burning of stockpiles of tusks to send a message that it will stop the ivory trade.

I am a student in China, which has the biggest ivory market in the world. Many Chinese think ivory falls out naturally. In 2017, my country said it was stopping the legal commercial processing and sale of ivory. I've never seen a living elephant but I learn about them from celebrities, social media apps and a virtual reality elephant.

I am Africa and some of my southern countries say their elephant populations are fine and so ivory sales would support their conservation efforts. Some of my other countries say that letting ivory trading start again would put their elephants in too much danger.

I am an anti-poaching dog. I scare poachers because I'm trained to sniff them out, and attack. Sometimes my handler and I parachute in to the front lines. I'm low technology and just want a pat for working hard.

I am Sri Lanka and in 2016, I became the first South Asian country to destroy its stockpile of ivory. I was also the first country in the world to issue a formal apology for its role in the ivory trade.

I'm eBay, a multinational e-commerce corporation. An investigation found I sold 2275 elephant ivory items in one week, and so I banned all sales of elephant-ivory products.

I am a drone. I have anti-poaching technology with multiple sensors and cameras. I'm cheap, cover big areas quickly, beam back live video transmission, and use infrared and thermal imaging to work in the dark, which is when poachers like to operate.

I am a park ranger in Africa. I investigate poaching crimes and track and catch poachers. I plan and carry out undercover operations and run informants. I'm lucky as I have a vehicle, weapon and communications technology; in some countries, park rangers don't even have boots to wear.

I am a poacher, which means I hunt and kill elephants even though it's against the law. I didn't go to school and I learnt how to be a poacher from my father. It's the only job I've had. Some villagers lace watering holes with cyanide to suffocate elephants but I use night-vision goggles and my rifle, and then I hack off the tusks.

I'm the Wildlife Conservation Society. One time, I crushed confiscated ivory from dealers and retailers in New York's Times Square to send a message that we won't allow the illegal trade of ivory to continue.

I am a treaty called CITES — the Convention on International Trade in Endangered Species of Wild Fauna and Flora. I have banned countries from trading in ivory.

ISBN: 9780170418409

SKILLS PRACTICE

1 Captioning

Make your own copy of this and add captions (short descriptions) to each image to describe what is happening.

2 Word clouding

Create a word cloud (image made up of different-sized and different-coloured words) about how people are working to save elephants.

3 Creative writing

Create a poem or short story for younger students that could accompany this image to convince them poaching is a bad idea.

4 Problem-solving

Make a list of questions you could give a think tank (group of experts) working on saving the elephants. (How to stop people buying products made of Ivory? Would painting tusks pink help?)

5 Choosing

Choose which of the two images would make the best poster for your school noticeboard and give at least one reason for your choice.

ISBN: 9780170418409

Eat the pests

- Lionfish get their name from their flaring spines.
- They are now found in the eastern Atlantic, far from their native South Pacific, Indian Ocean and Red Sea.
- They got there from people emptying aquariums.
- In their native areas, lionfish are controlled by predators such as sharks but elsewhere, predators ignore them so their numbers explode.
- They prey on local fish, and one lionfish can reduce fish biomass on a reef by 80 percent in one month.
- In places like Florida, local fish keep reefs healthy by clearing it of algae, so when lionfish prey on local fish, reefs die.
- Marine biologists say lionfish are like climate change — a top threat.
- Lionfish are not poisonous for humans to eat. Their spines are venomous, meaning they can sting you, but the venom is neutralised in cooking.

Making humans the top predator of lionfish is a way to fight back, so people are encouraged to catch them so they can eat them. This means creating a demand for the fish. Dive centres and diving organisations hold culls, derbies and hunts.

In 2017, 11th Hour Racing #EatLionfish Chefs' Throwdown was developed in collaboration with the British America's Cup Team Land Rover BAR in Bermuda to raise awareness about the environmental threat posed by lionfish. It featured celebrity chefs representing the six nations and teams competing in the America's Cup. Annabel Langbein from New Zealand was one. They served up lionfish delicacies, which were said to be a sustainable and tasty seafood. Chefs were chosen to take part for their skills and also their dedication to sustainable food sources. The MC was known as the Godfather of Sustainability. The winner was Sir Richard Branson's Necker Island head chef with three sustainable dishes of ceviche, lionfish coconut curry, and fish and chips.

RISE — Robots in Service of the Environment — focuses on developing robot technology to solve some of the world's most challenging environmental problems on a massive scale. Its first project was to develop an undersea robot to allow the mass capture of lionfish below depths that sport divers could reach. The Guardian LF1 submersible robot was developed using technology by iRobot. It could catch lionfish remotely at depths up to 122 metres using a controller similar to a gaming controller. It was the first device to reach, stun and capture lionfish found at depths below what is safe for divers.

ISBN: 9780170418409

SKILLS PRACTICE

1 Adapting (changing so it becomes better suited)

Adapt the image to show the interconnection among reef fish, humans and lionfish.

2 Paragraph construction

Use the following notes to construct a paragraph about a new app.

> ***Florida's Invasive Species Management Tools include the Report Lion Fish App. App developed for Florida Fish and Wildlife Conservation Commission. FWC encourages people to remove lionfish in Florida. Smart device app unveiled during live Twitter chat. First 250 people to complete Report Florida Lionfish app reporting form got free interactive Lionfish Control Team T-shirt. Logo designed to come to life. Has info about lionfish, safe handling guidelines, take pictures, report sightings or harvests.***

3 Deducing

> ***'Sustainability ______________________ I am consciously aware of issues around things like keeping our oceans clean and all sorts of issues about how we consume. Lionfish are a predatory fish that breed like crazy and eat up all the good fish that help protect the coral.' (Annabel Langbein)***

Some of the speaker's opening sentence is missing. From what you know of her and the rest of her comments here, which one of the following is most likely the missing words? Say why.

a runs opposite to all I believe in.
b is very close to my heart.
c has little to do with this issue.

4 Convincing

You have identified a demand in the pet canned-food market for a fresh source of whole-meat protein and think lionfish would be excellent. List ideas you could use to convince someone to provide funds for you to start up a business.

5 Headlining

In June 2016, a new study showed that the first wave of a lionfish invasion had struck in the Mediterranean Sea, a region where the fish had not been established before.
Create three different headlines for a news story about this.

ISBN: 9780170418409

Kaitiaki for Aotearoa

Humans in Aotearoa have affected and continue to affect the environment. For example, Maori hunted moa to extinction and Pakeha removed much of the kauri.

One traditional (long-established) Maori idea that is being adopted more and more by all New Zealanders is kaitiakitanga.

Kaitiakitanga says:

- there is a relation between humans and the environment
- humans are part of the environment but do not own it
- if something is wrong with the environment, such as a river being polluted, there will be something not right with the local people
- a kaitiaki is a person or group whom iwi see as a guardian of a particular place or resource (a useful or valuable thing), such as a hapu (sub-tribe) being a kaitiaki for a lake
- a kaitiaki has the responsibility of protecting the mauri (life force) of the place or resource and passing it on to future generations in an undamaged condition
- it lets modern Maori feel they are following the responsibilities and hopes of their ancestors and lets non-Maori see how it can help the environment.

Examples of kaitiakitangi in action today

Deforestation and land development around the Waiapu River in the Gisborne district causes erosion, which puts into the river a lot of sediment — soil that settles into the water. Every year millions of tonnes of this soil go out to the ocean. In 2014, Ngati Porou, as kaitiaki, and the Crown signed agreements which included targeting erosion control of the river. The vision was healthy land, healthy rivers, healthy people — Ko te mana: Ko te hauora o te whenua, ko te hauora o nga awa, ko te hauora o te iwi.

Government returned the rights of pounamu (greenstone) ownership to Te Rūnanga o Ngāi Tahu, Ngai Tahu iwi's tribal council. As kaitiaki, Ngai Tahu has the responsibility of making sure pounamu is managed sustainably. This means not just caring for the stone but also protecting the rivers from which it comes.

Ngati Hine iwi in Northland use the term kukupa for the native wood pigeon, which have declined in the Motatau Forest. DOC said Te Runanga o Ngati Hine were co-managers with it of the Motatau Forest and with traditional Maori and non-Maori management, such as putting a rahui (ban) on kukupa, and getting rid of pests, the kukupa population of the Motatau area more than doubled.

ISBN: 9780170418409

In the past, hundreds of tuatara were shipped to overseas museums and collectors until the species become one of the first natives to be protected by law. Modern smugglers get big money for tuatara overseas and they are recognised as a species that needs active conservation management. The Karori Sanctuary became home to the mainland's only wild population of tuatara when 70 were transferred from Stephens Island (Takapourewa) with the blessing of the animals' kaitiaki, Ngati Koata.

SKILLS PRACTICE

1 Representing an idea

State which one you think best represents the idea of kaitiakitanga and why.

2 Sorting true (tika) from false (kahore)

Copy out the true statements about kaitiakitanga. Then turn the false statements into true ones and copy them out also.

- **a** It offers no help for non-Maori efforts to protect the environment.
- **b** It is a modern Maori idea.
- **c** It is a response to issues and challenges.
- **d** It sees humans as separate to the environment.
- **e** It is about guarding places and resources.
- **f** It has nothing to do with sustainability.
- **g** It is linked to both the past and the future.

3 Defining official language

Explain what the underlined words mean.

New Zealand's Resource Management Act says that people managing resources under the Act must take notice of kaitiakitanga. The Act defines kaitiakitanga as 'the exercise of guardianship by the tangata whenua of an area in accordance with tikanga Maori in relation to natural and physical resources; and includes the ethic of stewardship'.

4 Freehand sketching

Sketch an outline map of New Zealand and mark in the approximate area of the four examples of kaitiakitanga. Make the marks broad circles. For example, Ngati Koata and Takapourewa are at the top of the South Island, and Karori is in Wellington. Give the map a title, frame and key.

5 Reasoning

How many reasons can you offer to explain why such a cartoon would not have appeared a hundred years ago?

Shoot-to-kill or fine?

Many individuals and companies acting against the environment haven't been caught, or have escaped punishment. Increasingly, however, countries are passing laws to catch and punish. Even China, regularly named as one of the biggest polluters on the planet, recently revised its laws to get polluting companies named and shamed, individuals imprisoned and fined, and local government officials fired and demoted. Other countries have different approaches. In Kaziranga National Park in India, rangers have the licence to shoot on sight rhino poachers. The man who introduced the controversial policy said he thought environmental crimes were more serious than murder. Results of the policy include the killing of poachers, the killing of innocent villagers along park borders, and the growth in rhino numbers.

Getting tougher

1. In 2017, New Zealand strengthened DOC rangers' powers to protect native wildlife from poaching and smuggling by allowing them to take more action, such as seizing evidence like laptops, cameras and mobile phones. DOC's specialist enforcement officers could arrest for serious offending against absolutely protected wildlife involving illegal hunting, killing or export.
2. Recently, DOC announced changes to the protection status of more than 50 species. For example, if you killed a katipo, New Zealand's most venomous spider, you could be in serious trouble because it has 'absolute protection', as the kereru (kukupa) and kiwi have. The maximum penalty for killing creatures with absolute protection is a year in prison or a $100,000 fine.

Examples of punishment for environmental crimes

2002 Fletcher Concrete and Infrastructure fined nearly $29,000 for a series of toxic discharges into Papakura Stream, which flows into Manukau Harbour.

2005 Three Otago farmers fined $2500 for killing a fur seal on the Otago coast.

2007 South African fined $5000 for trying to smuggle 44 parrot eggs out of Auckland.

2009 Man got 14 weeks' imprisonment and a $5000 fine for trying to smuggle 24 geckos and 20 skinks out of Christchurch Airport.

2010 Fonterra fined $24,000 for a chemical spill at its Edgecumbe milk processing plant.

2010 German tourist sentenced to 12 weeks in jail for trying to smuggle 44 geckos and skinks in his underwear out of Christchurch Airport.

2010 Two people jailed for 18 weeks for taking jewelled geckos from Otago.

2012 A Canterbury farm manager fined $20,000 and sentenced to 260 hours of community service for discharging effluent (liquid waste or sewage discharged into water such as rivers or the sea) into a Lake Ellesmere waterway.

ISBN: 9780170418409

2015 Fonterra fined $362,000 over odorous compounds coming out of Eltham Wastewater Treatment Plant and for discharging buttermilk in a South Taranaki treatment pond that caused a stench. The South Taranaki District Council had already pleaded guilty to a charge for its part in the stench and been fined $115,000.

2016 Fonterra fined over $170,000 for polluting Rangitaiki River, through failures of its waste water irrigation system, overflows into the stormwater system and whey dumped into the river.

2016 Three Bay of Plenty farmers fined from $12,000 to more than $26,000 for breaching effluent discharge conditions.

2016 Mobil Oil New Zealand fined $288,000 for oil spill into Tauranga Harbour.

2016 Man fined $24,500 and sentenced to community detention and community work for killing and smuggling kereru on a flight from Invercargill to Northland.

SKILLS PRACTICE

1 Looking at differences

State the following.

- **a** Three different ways the location of the park is shown.
- **b** Three differences you might expect between it and a New Zealand national park.

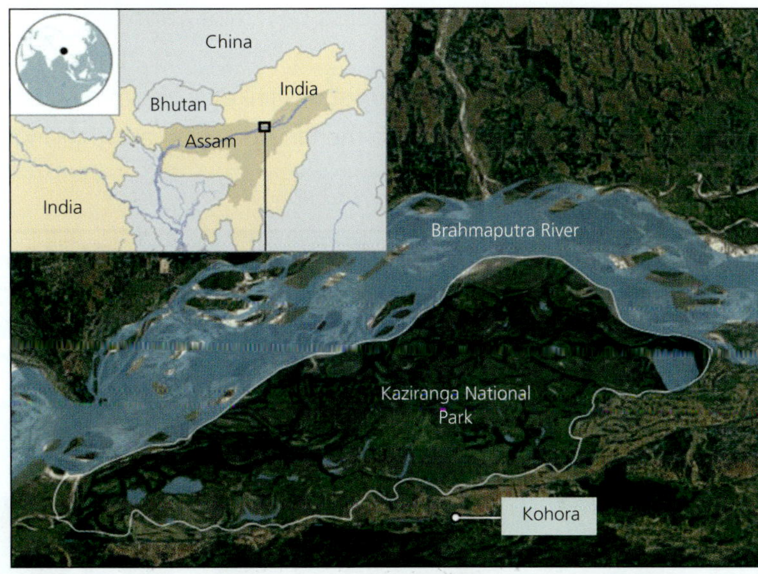

2 Naming

In April 2017, Otago Museum invited the public to supply a name for a rare native jewelled gecko. It was smuggled to Germany in 2013 and later rescued and nursed back to health at Wellington Zoo. It could not be released into the wild because it could have been exposed to biosecurity threats overseas and so it ended up at Otago Museum.

State what name you would have suggested. Give the reasoning behind your name choice.

3 Designing

- **a** State if you would wear this T-shirt and give a reason for your answer.
- **b** Design a T-shirt that has a message for environmental polluters.

4 Relating to national identity

'Our birds, our animals and our forests are central to our sense of our national identity. They are our national monuments, taonga that are treasured by all New Zealanders.' (Maggie Barry, Minister of Conservation)

State the following.

a What she means.

b Whether you agree or not, and why or why not.

c The type of punishments used in New Zealand for environmental crimes.

d How these differ to the one at Kaziranga and what you think about the Kaziranga policy.

5 Being neutral

Background = In August of 2013, Fonterra recalled products after it found a suspected botulism-causing bacteria during safety tests. The products had been sold to make infant formula and sports drinks. No cases of sick consumers were reported although China put a temporary ban on importing. The botulism scare turned out to be a false alarm.

Think about how the cartoonist has linked a present scare to a different ongoing pollution issue. Show how he has done this. State the facts only and avoid giving your own opinion on the scare and issue.

 ISBN: 9780170418409

The debate over freedom camping

38

Unofficial definition of freedom camping

- Staying at a place that is not an official camp site.
- Liked by travellers because it is free.
- If done in a prohibited (banned) or restricted area, can result in a fine.
- Often means no access to facilities such as toilets and waste disposal.
- Attracts criticism because waste is left.

Official definition of freedom camping

(From the New Zealand Freedom Camping Act 2011)

Meaning of freedom camp

1 In this Act, freedom camp means to camp (other than at a camping ground) within 200m of a motor vehicle accessible area or the mean low-water springs line of any sea or harbour, or on or within 200m of a formed road or a Great Walks Track, using one or more of the following:

- **a** a tent or other temporary structure;
- **b** a caravan;
- **c** a car, campervan, housetruck, or other motor vehicle.

2 In this Act, freedom camping does not include the following activities:

- **a** temporary and short-term parking of a motor vehicle;
- **b** recreational activities commonly known as day-trip excursions;
- **c** resting or sleeping at the roadside in a caravan or motor vehicle to avoid driver fatigue.

Opinions about freedom camping

1. It causes conflict between locals and visitors.
2. It mucks up the environment and our clean and green image.
3. Cars and minivans aren't safe for camping, cooking and sleeping in.
4. It shows no respect for the environment.
5. We need to find a solution so visitors are made to feel welcome and we protect our environment.
6. It might be free camping but it costs ratepayers who have to clean up rubbish.
7. It helps the economies of many small towns.
8. We need to sort out the problem without banning it because of the few ratbags.
9. Councils should provide bathroom facilities at all major pull-off areas.
10. Some freedom campers won't use nearby toilets because they're in such bad condition.
11. Freedom campers park in free car parks next to clubhouses and so there's no space for members.
12. We should have stricter penalties such as deporting them.

ISBN: 9780170418409

SKILLS PRACTICE 

1 Attitudes

Use numbers to list which opinions (page 101) are in support, which are neutral, and which are against.

2 Clarity

- **a** What do you think this sign means?
- **b** State which version, the unofficial definition or the official definition, tells you more clearly what freedom camping means, and why you think that.

3 Understanding complications

A complication is something that can make you rethink an issue. New Zealand's housing crisis has seen some people living in cars or parks because of high rents. Explain how that could be a complication for the public perception of (way of looking at) freedom campers.

4 Reading a graph

- **a** To what do the two sets of data refer?
- **b** Why are there two lines for each set of data?
- **c** For the three-year average, about how many freedom campers were there in the early 2000s and how did that compare to about 15 years later?
- **d** Does it make a difference to your reaction to the increase in numbers if you learn that those more recent freedom campers made up only around 2 percent of the total number of visitors to New Zealand? Give a reason for your answer.
- **e** About how much did three-year-average freedom campers spend in the early 2000s and how did that compare to about 15 years later?
- **f** Does it make a difference to your reaction to the increase in spending if you learn that freedom campers spent more than the average international visitor? Give a reason for your answer.

5 Context (background events that form setting and help understanding)

Background = Reports that a large recreation site was planned for earthquake-damaged land in Christchurch East where red zone refers to an area the public is not allowed to enter because of safety issues.

Explain how the cartoonist has used context.

 ISBN: 9780170418409

The rise and rise of ecotourism

- Ecotourism is the fastest-growing part of global tourism.
- The International Ecotourism Society (TIES) defines ecotourism as 'responsible travel to natural areas that conserves the environment and improves the wellbeing of local people'.
- The United Nations made 2017 the International Year of Sustainable Tourism for Development.

It looks as if this hiker walking through rainforest treetops in Malaysia could be a 100 percent ecotourist. However, if he or anyone else in his tour group damages the environment in any way, such as tossing rubbish into the treetops, it is not true ecotourism. And if the community in whose territory he is walking does not earn any money from his visit — for example, by supplying food and lodging — it is not true ecotourism. A bonus to him is that the local people might share sustainable methods they have been using for generations. A bonus to the community is it earns money, which will stop it resorting to unsustainable actions such as animal poaching.

Ecolodging is about highlighting the location and sustainable qualities of the accommodation. For example, by staying in a Mongolian ger in the Gobi Desert, you get to learn about tents made of animal hide and fur that herders have been using for thousands of years, as well as learning about the local environment. Ecolodges have features such as renewable energy, waste reduction, composting, organic gardens, and conserving native vegetation.

Ecotrekking is about travelling as locals do. A local guide might supervise the trek and provide information about the environment.

ISBN: 9780170418409

Blue Flag Global is an eco-label certification programme that ensures quality in sustainability efforts in coastal environments. It has awarded certification to sites in about 50 different countries all over the world, including New Zealand. Spain has more Blue Flag awards than any other country.

Environmentally friendly travel to Machu Picchu in Peru

- Respect local efforts to protect their environment from tourist overload such as managers of Machu Picchu setting out a permit system to control the number of trekkers on the Inca Trail.
- Use public transport and if travel by air is unavoidable, use a carbon-offsetting scheme such as planting trees to make up for the carbon dioxide released by air travel.
- Use eco-friendly home accommodation where hosts have to make sure their homes embrace sustainability.
- Use eco-friendly hotel accommodation. Famous hotel brands are now appointing senior management positions to oversee sustainability practices and use systems to manage waste, water, air and energy.

SKILLS PRACTICE

1 Creating a chart

Make a chart to show the rights and responsibilities of the ecotourist.

2 Understanding win-win

Explain why ecotourism can be a win-win situation for hosts and tourists.

ISBN: 9780170418409

3 Acknowledging

You are compiling a series of cartoons about how the growth of ecotourism might impact on the environment. State the following.

a Why this Alastair Nisbet cartoon would make an excellent example.

b Why you must acknowledge the cartoonist, date and where the cartoon was published.

Alastair Nisbet, December 2005, published in The Press.

4 Referencing

With over 20 percent of it covered in national parks, forest areas and reserves, along with its huge coastline, New Zealand has a great opportunity ...

Write out the sentence and complete it with a reference to ecotourism.

5 Innovating (doing something new)

Study the cartoon and state how it suggests that innovation can create both opportunities and challenges for people and places.

Background = A report for Hamilton councillors recommended creating a Maori village on an island in the Waikato with flying fox and artificial surfing as tourist attractions.

Activists act for change

Environmental activist = person who works to bring about positive change such as getting people to march in a show of support for the environment. Every year, more than 100 environmental activists are murdered.

Rachel Carson Wildlife Sanctuary in Maine, USA.

- Santctuary established to protect salt marshes and estuaries for migratory birds.
- Named after Rachel Carson (1907–64), an American who is regarded as an early environmental activist.
- Her most famous book, *Silent Spring*, was about how general human pollution and specific use of insecticides such as DDT was killing birds.

- Earth Day celebrated each 22 April around the world for people to show they understand their responsibility to create a clean and safe environment.
- Named by American politician Gaylord Nelson, who was inspired to create it after seeing a massive oil spill off the coast of California.
- The oil spill area became ground zero for many conservation efforts.

Examples of actions

1. The People's Climate March on 21 September 2014 in New York City was about asking for global action against climate change. The estimated 400,000 marchers made it the largest climate change march in history.
2. Blockadia is a term used for camps set up by activists trying to block a pipeline in Texas with their bodies. The Blockadia movement now fights fossil fuel extraction around the world either physically or legally such as indigenous people using traditional land rights and treaties to resist huge corporations and governments.
3. French anti-fracking activists have a slogan, *Ni ici, ni ailleurs*, meaning *Not here, nor anywhere*. France was the first country to ban fracking for extracting natural gas. There is a growing list of countries, states, cities, towns and regions doing the same.
4. The fight to preserve forests in Greece became a national cause linked to the movement against fossil fuels generally and specifically against making a huge open-pit gold mine in Halkidiki in northern Greece. Activists said the mine would cause massive deforestation and was above the region's main aquifer.

  ISBN: 9780170418409

Examples of activists

1 Severn Cullis-Suzuki, born in 1979 in Canada, was nine years old when she founded the Environmental Children's Organization (ECO), a group of children dedicated to learning and teaching others about environmental issues. At age 12, she raised money with ECO to attend the Rio Earth Summit where she presented environmental issues from a youth perspective. The video of that became a viral hit, and she became known as The Girl Who Silenced the World for 5 Minutes. Today she speaks around the world on environmental issues, and asks people to act with the future in mind.
2 Prince Charles, born in 1948 as a member of the British Royal Family, has launched many sustainability actions, such as the International Sustainability Unit, and The Prince's Rainforests Project, to help find solutions that work.
3 Wangari Maathai (1940–2011) of Kenya set up the Green Belt Movement, which organised females in rural Kenya to plant trees for the environment. She was the first African woman to receive the Nobel Peace Prize.
4 Daryl Hannah, born in 1960, is an American actress and an active environmentalist who has her own weekly video blog on sustainable solutions. Her home runs on solar power and is built with green materials, and her car runs on biodiesel. She has been arrested and spent time in jail for her environmental opposition and is a member of the World Future Council.

An example from New Zealand

Lake Manapouri, in New Zealand's Fiordland National Park, seemed to be a good location for a hydro-electric power station but the idea was to raise the lake level, which many people opposed. The Save Manapouri campaign began and a petition went to Parliament. The lake level was not raised. This was the first time Kiwis had successfully fought a big development on environmental grounds and it helped raise environmental awareness.

SKILLS PRACTICE

1 Finding an image

Find an image to go with one of the following quotes you are using to make a poster.

The activist cleans the world rather than moans how dirty it is.
The oceans are rising and so are we.
There is no Planet B.
Be an agent of change.
Everybody needs to get involved.
Go green to get the globe clean.
Don't be mean, be green.
May the forest be with you.
Hug a tree; they have fewer issues than people.

2 Writing a note

Run a competition to see if anyone can come up with a better environmental note to future generations than this one.

Dear future generations: Please accept our apologies.
We were rolling drunk on petroleum.
(Kurt Vonnegut)

3 Thinking of your future

Imagine you are an environmental activist.

a Which world leader would you most like to meet for a talk about the environment?

b Which place would you like named after you or by you?

4 Criteria (standards by which you can judge)

You have been given several cartoons such as the one here to judge for how well they show environmental activism.

a State what criteria you will use. An example could be the definition of activism.

b Is this cartoon showing environmental activism? Say why or why not.

Man, I'm feeling good. We saved eighty bucks in taxes by defeating that environmental initiative.

5 Giving examples

Choose one of the following and give some examples of it in action.

- Ideas and actions of people in the past can have impact.
- People view and use places differently.

ISBN: 9780170418409

Eco-terrorists or eco-warriors?

People who carry out acts of violence to protect the environment and change the way people behave towards it are called eco-terrorists by some and eco-warriors by others. Actions include tree spiking (hammering a spike into a tree, which will damage a chainsaw although it could also damage the logger), arson, spiking roads, disabling vehicles, vandalising buildings, delivering sewage or dead animals to offices as protests, plugging waste discharge pipes, graffiti, destroying experiments such as a test plot of genetically modified wheat, and cutting drift nets.

Examples

1 A group of Kayapo Indian warriors, wanting to protect the Amazon rainforest against goldminers, travelled more than 200 kilometres by boat and on foot to the illegal mining camps where they destroyed mining equipment.

2 Giant mining corporation Rio Tinto Zinc decided to increase production at Panguna Mine on the island of Bougainville in Papua New Guinea. Locals were sick of their environment getting damaged. They formed the Bougainville Revolutionary Army (BRA), stole explosives from the mine and blew up supply lines and burned other equipment including a helicopter. This stopped production at the mine. When the Papua New Guinea Army arrived, BRA fought them off with bows and arrows and sticks and stones. The PNG Army imposed a gunboat blockade around Bougainville to stop supplies. They thought BRA would give in within a few weeks. But they were surprised to see locals still driving their vehicles. The locals were using coconut oil as fuel. The affair lasted eight years until international peace negotiations forced PNG to back down.

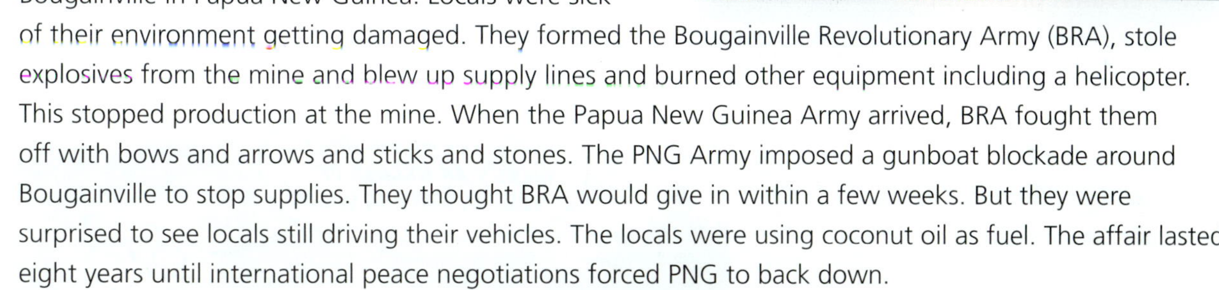

3 Anti-oil activists Liberate Tate tried to stop the Tate Art Gallery getting funding from petroleum company BP. Their actions included covering a naked man with oil, carrying a 1.5-tonne wind turbine blade into the gallery's main hall, and releasing a sound artwork themed around BP sponsorship of Tate, which was downloaded onto smartphones, iPods and MP3 players and played while their owners walked around the Tate London galleries.

4 Julia Butterfly Hill spent 738 days in a 55-metre tall, about 1500-year-old California redwood tree, known as Luna, to stop loggers cutting it down. She used solar-powered cellphones for radio interviews, became an in-tree correspondent for a TV show, pulled up supplies that her support team brought her and cooked on a small stove. She survived freezing rains, El Nino winds, a helicopter bothering her, the anger of loggers and security guards, and agreed to get out of the tree only when the logging company agreed to preserve Luna and some other trees. The money that she and activists raised went to the logging company, which donated it to a university for research into sustainable forestry.

ISBN: 9780170418409

5 A project to transport crude oil from North Dakota to a refinery in Illinois had a pipeline that would travel underneath the Missouri River. Standing Rock Sioux tribe have a reservation in the area and thousands of Native American supporters set up camps to try to block the project because they said it threatened native lands, leaks could pollute the water supply from the Missouri River, and it would contribute to man-made climate change by building up oil infrastructure. In 2017, when oil began flowing through the pipeline, four Sioux tribes had a lawsuit waiting.

6 Greenpeace angered the Peruvian government when some of its activists trekked through Peru's ancient Nazca Lines, a UNESCO World Heritage site not open to the public, to stage a publicity stunt timed to coincide with UN climate change talks being held in Peru's capital of Lima. The Nazca Lines are a collection of hundreds of large designs such as animals, people, shapes and flowers that indigenous people etched into the ground over 1500 years ago. Officials released drone footage showing the damage activists did by putting their Time for Change! sign next to a design and accidentally creating new path lines.

SKILLS PRACTICE

1 Explaining difference

Use two of the images (page 109) to help you explain your thoughts on the difference between environmental activism (Unit 40) and eco-terrorism.

2 Debating

Prepare some ideas about whether eco-terrorism is good or bad for the environment. Think about society and the economy as well.

3 Personal preference

State whether, and why, you would prefer to be a tree-sitter, a tree-hugger, a tree-logger or a tree-spiker.

4 Using an idea

This cartoon refers to the anonymous blackmail threat over 1080 use, which the Prime Minister said was eco-terrorism. State how the cartoonist has used the idea of eco-terrorism.

5 Gauging difficulty

The US FBI defines eco-terrorism as 'the use or threatened use of violence of a criminal nature against people or property by an environmentally oriented, subnational group for environmental-political reasons, or aimed at an audience beyond the target, often of a symbolic nature.'

State how difficult you find that to understand and why you think the FBI wrote it in such a way.

ISBN: 9780170418409

Lab-grown meat muscling towards your plate

Lab-grown meat, also called cultured meat or synthetic meat, is meat grown in a cell culture instead of meat grown inside animals.

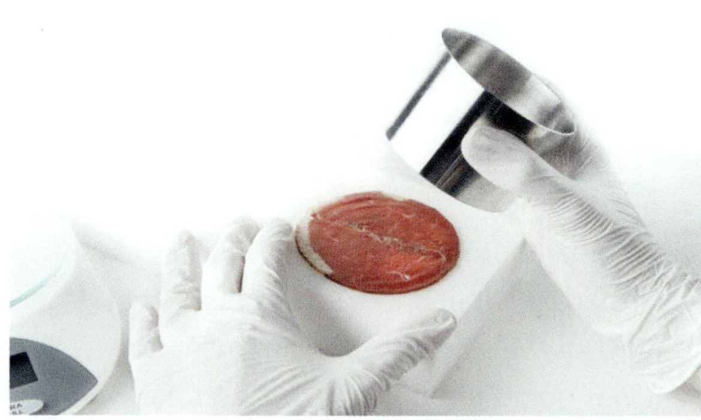

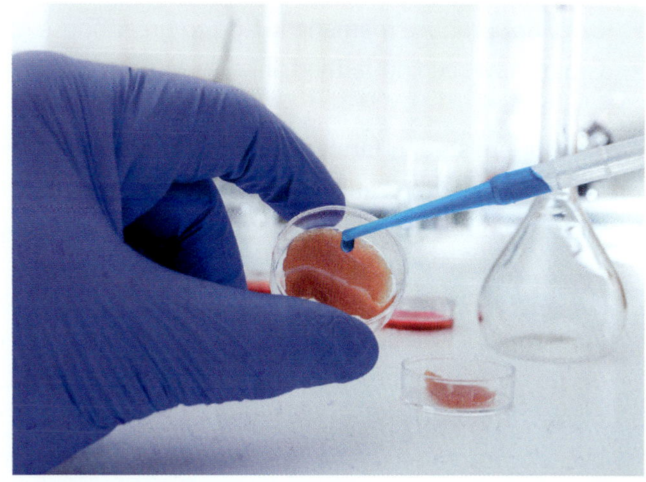

The Dutch Cultured Meat Project aimed to show the world that it was scientifically possible to create an edible beef burger from cultured cells.

The first cultured beef burger patty was created in the Netherlands. The scientists' resources were a few bits of muscle from cows. The scientists used those to make a burger patty by mincing about 20,000 strands they grew in the lab, and mixing them with salt, breadcrumbs, egg powder and natural red colorants.

In front of a live television audience including 200 journalists from around the world and the academics who worked on the Dutch Cultured Meat Project, in London on 5 August 2013, a chef cooked the patty, and then three people tasted it. It did not get rave reviews for its taste but by 2017 the general agreement was that lab-grown meat was on its way to plates, which would help the environment by it not having to keep up with the global demand for animal-grown meat.

ISBN: 9780170418409

Environmental advantages

- Needs less food input (instead of growing a whole animal, you grow only the muscle).
- Needs less land (could be grown in city skyscrapers).
- Needs less water (you can use microscopic algae instead of water).
- Produces less waste (no solid waste, as you grow exactly what you want).
- Cleaner (a lab can be kept sterile; a farm cannot).
- Helps fight climate change and global warming.
- Land used for agriculture can go back to its natural state.
- Does not produce methane to add to greenhouse gas emissions.
- Grains now feeding farmed animals could instead feed people.

In 2017, scientists and farmers took part in the Agricultural Greenhouse Gas Mitigation Conference in Manawatu. There the Parliamentary Commissioner for the Environment said New Zealand farmers should beware of synthetic meat and milk being developed by California's Silicon Valley.

In 2016, diners in San Francisco, New York and Los Angeles got hamburgers that took five years to create. Although they were made entirely from plants, they tasted, smelt and looked like beef. They sizzled, browned and oozed fat while they cooked. The founder of the start-up company in Silicon Valley that created the burgers said global demand for meat was going through the roof and the world was not going to be able to satisfy it because it did not have enough space or water.

SKILLS PRACTICE

1 Circles comparing

a Make a general comment about the structure of the comparison.

b Make a more detailed comment about what it shows.

c State which percentage you would expect to go down as the technology for lab-grown beef improves and why.

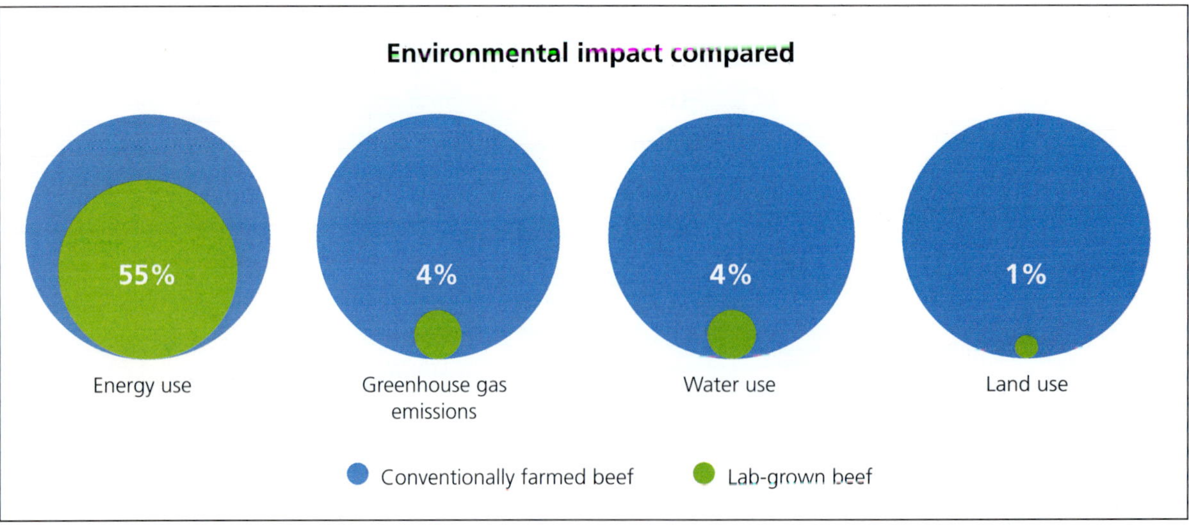

ISBN: 9780170418409

2 Visualising

State what the New Zealand environment might look like if farming for meat production was reduced or stopped.

3 Using headlines to guess content

After the first lab-meat patty was made, headlines such as the following began to appear around the world.

Lab-grown meat rebranded clean meat to address yuk factor

Australia exhibits 3D-printed meat

Chef cooks world's first lab-grown chicken

Meet world's first cultured meatball

Lab-grown meat is in your future

Lab-grown meat coming to supermarket shelves

Many start-ups aiming to disrupt meat industry

Make your own meat with open-source cells

For each headline, state what you think the article was about.

4 Placements

State where in the text you would put the following, and why.

Later the creator said, 'The first burger was created in a petri dish but a bioreactor the size of an Olympic swimming pool could feed 40,000 people for a year.'

'It was a major challenge,' she said. 'We know how fast they can develop things.' The Commissioner was right.

It's close to meat but not all that juicy, was an opinion.

The world eats seven times more animals than it did in 1950.

5 Looking at possibilities

a Explain why there are different possibilities for population in 2100, what they are, and how the graph shows them.

b Explain why this graph would be of interest to a person thinking of investing in a start-up for lab-grown meat production.

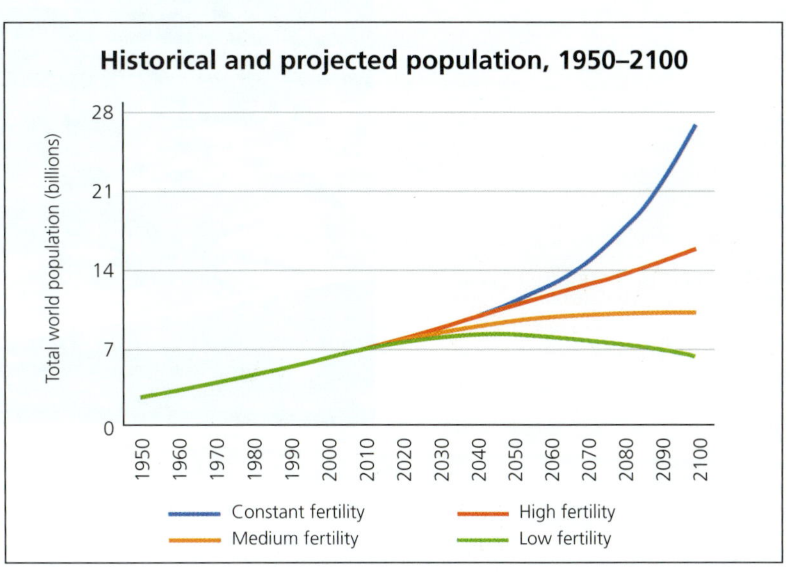

ISBN: 9780170418409

Tickling taste

- Over two billion people around the world regularly eat insects by choice but many Westerners are not keen.
- However, most people have eaten insects as insect parts are legally in items such as flour, orange juice, frozen broccoli.
- Futurologists say entomophagy (insect-eating) will be something the whole world does by design, not by accident.
- Many people first try something like a candy and protein shake made from insects, or sky prawns (fried locusts) on a dare but then get a taste for it.
- Insects are appearing on menus at many establishments in many countries including New Zealand.
- Consumers are told that with just one meal a week of insect protein instead of conventional meat, they help the environment by saving land, carbon emissions and water.
- Entrepreneurs see them as a good investment. Rapper NAS invested in US start-up Exo, a company that makes protein bars with added crushed-up crickets.
- The world is learning about insect superfoods. Chicken is 23 percent protein but crickets are about 65 percent and they are also full of zinc, manganese and potassium, and a 20-gram serve gives half the daily recommended intake of calcium and iron.

Nearly 2000 species are edible, with low percentage of wasted parts.

Cheap and reliable protein, fats, carbohydrates, minerals, vitamins.

Need no insecticides and little feed and water to grow.

Insect farming is low-tech and inexpensive.

Need little space and can be farmed vertically.

Can be farmed on a large scale and cope with living in high densities.

Have fast growth and breeding and are easy to kill humanely.

Produce fewer greenhouse gases and flatulence than farmed animals.

ISBN: 9780170418409

From pest to food

When parts of Australia were struggling to deal with the worst locust plague in 30 years, a new cookbook came out — *Cooking with Sky Prawns* — with more than 20 locust recipes. They included locust dumplings, chocolate-covered locusts, and locust-flavoured popcorn. One of the authors said, 'If you've eaten a lobster, crab or crayfish, you've already eaten Arthropoda, of which insects are part. So popping a big, juicy locust in your mouth is only a step away.'

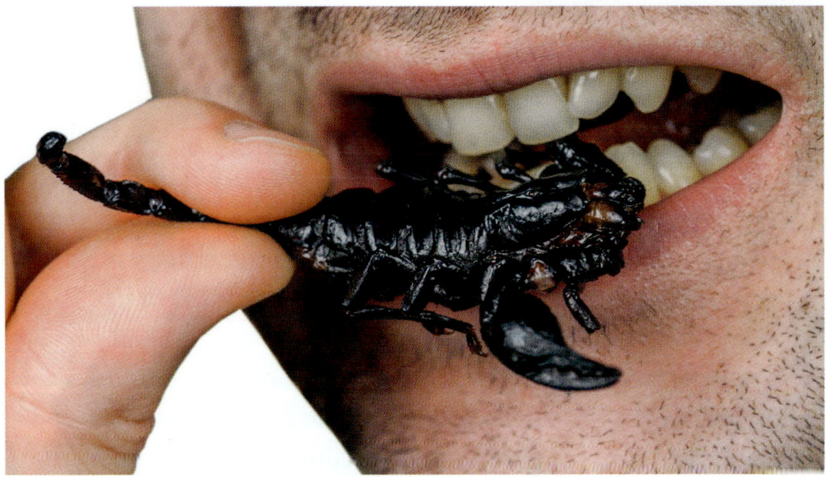

The Wildfoods Festival in the West Coast town of Hokitika has become a special event in New Zealand. New wild foods are introduced every year. Examples are wasp larvae ice cream, scorpions (raw and cooked), chocolate worm truffles, worm sushi and worm dukkha.

SKILLS PRACTICE

1 Personal response

- **a** State which of the responses is closest to your own about eating insects, and why.
- **b** State how your culture influenced your answer.

2 Questionnaire

- **a** Create a questionnaire of six questions about eating insects by deciding what information you want and writing the questions to get it.
- **b** Give your questionnaire to six people.
- **c** Summarise the results of your questionnaire.

3 Expressing opinions

Write down your opinions and some ideas on the following two questions that you could use in a discussion.

If competitive cooking shows on New Zealand television offered insects in the pantry instead of conventional meat, would people still want to compete in them and would viewers still watch?

Will your children have a different attitude to eating insects than your generation has?

4 Noting main ideas

'It is widely accepted that by 2050 the world will host nine billion people. To accommodate this number, current food production will need to almost double. Land is scarce and expanding the area devoted to farming is rarely a viable or sustainable option. Oceans are overfished and climate change and related water shortages could have profound implications for food production. To meet the food and nutrition challenges of today — there are nearly one billion chronically hungry people worldwide — and tomorrow, what we eat and how we produce it needs to be re-evaluated. Inefficiencies need to be rectified and food waste reduced. We need to find new ways of growing food. Edible insects have always been a part of human diets, but in some societies there is a degree of distaste for their consumption. Although the majority of edible insects are gathered from forest habitats, innovation in mass-rearing systems has begun in many countries. Insects offer a significant opportunity to merge traditional knowledge and modern science in both developed and developing countries.' (Food and Agriculture Organization of the United Nations [FAO])

Write the numbers 1 to 10 down your margin for the 10 sentences from FAO. For each sentence, note the main idea.

5 Translating data to graphs

For each of the following sets, draw a graph to show the data.

Kilograms of feed grain to yield 1 kg of live animal weight:
Chicken (2.5), Pig (5), Beef cattle (10), Insect (1.7).

Litres of water for 1 kg of protein:
Chicken (360), Pig (600), Beef cattle (1500), Cricket (1).

Edible percentage of whole animal:
Chicken (55), Pig (55), Beef cattle (40), Cricket (80).

Greenhouse gas emissions grams:
Chicken (300), Pig (1130), Beef cattle (2850), Insect (1).

ISBN: 9780170418409

Why muck up the environment to grow food nobody eats?

44

Wasted food = wasted water, wasted energy, wasted land, greenhouse gas emissions from production of wasted food, greenhouse gas emissions from disposal of wasted food, waste in landfills, …

An issue of confusion for some consumers is labels. Use by date is about safety. You can eat foods up until the use by date but not after because it may be unsafe to eat. Best before date is about quality, not safety. You could eat the food after the best before date but it may not taste as good.

The United Nations Environment Programme estimates that global food production creates at least 30 percent of greenhouse gas emissions, is the largest single driver of biodiversity loss, and accounts for 70 percent of fresh water use and 80 percent of deforestation.

Yet

About one third of food produced globally for human consumption every year gets lost or wasted, while 795 million people worldwide don't have enough to eat.

For example:
New Zealand families throw away \$872 million worth of food every year and the average household sends around 79 kg of edible food to landfills, while cafes, restaurants and supermarkets also throw away millions of dollars of food every year. Stopping this food waste would have the same effect as reducing CO_2 emissions by 325,975 tonnes, the equivalent of planting 130,390 trees or taking 118,107 fossil-fuelled cars off the road for a year.

ISBN: 9780170418409

The fight against wasting food

The United Nations Environment Programme is trying to accelerate action on reducing food waste. UN leaders have dined on food that would have been wasted to highlight how food waste is an overlooked aspect of climate change.

The community fridge movement began in Spain and spread to other countries including New Zealand. It encourages the public and businesses to leave edible and free food, which would go to waste, in a fridge in an urban area for people to eat.

The US goal of cutting food waste by 50 percent by 2030 was the first effort by a country to reduce food waste.

In Italy, a new set of laws aims to cut down food wastage. Families are encouraged to use doggy bags to take home unfinished food after eating out and it is easier for farmers and supermarkets to donate food to charity.

Supermarket chains in France are legally not allowed to destroy unsold food; owners face fines if they do not sign contracts with food donation charities for food fit for human consumption and farms for food fit for animal feed or compost.

STOP FOOD WASTING!

Community Fruit Harvesting is a network of volunteers that distributes fruit and jars of produce, has a marketplace on Facebook, and food rescue vans to connect those with excess food to those who need food.

The Love Food Hate Waste campaign began in the UK and got an 18 percent reduction in the amount of food discarded by households. New Zealand's Love Food Hate Waste campaign launched in 2016. Events have included the Great Persimmon Rescue when Waikato councils worked with volunteers and Community Fruit Harvesting to pick 20 tonnes of persimmons that would have been left to rot.

In the past, farmers might have discarded between 20 and 40 percent of their fresh produce because it did not meet retailers' cosmetic specifications — it did not look pretty. Some supermarkets have begun relaxing standards on fruit appearance, selling misshaped items for a reduced price and helping raise awareness that odd-shaped does not mean bad.

New technologies help. Improved storage bags in the Philippines helped cut losses of rice by 15 percent. In West Africa, use of solar dryers to extend the shelf life of fruit and tubers reduces losses.

Governments are looking at ways to smooth the process and give protection to food donors should products given away in good faith cause illness.

ISBN: 9780170418409

SKILLS PRACTICE

1 Supplying messages

State another five messages about food wastage this person might broadcast.

2 Creating cartoon frames

Create a third frame to show what happens next.

This portion size could challenge the throat capacity of a horse.

I'll pay double for half as much.

3 Snap polling

Use this question to snap poll 10 people. Show the results by either a written summary or a visual summary.

4 Understanding context

Study the cartoon and state the following.

a What is happening.

b What issue is supplying the context.

c What action the man might do next.

5 Matching

Write out these sentences about a community fridge and at the beginning of each sentence put one of How, When, Who, What, Why, Where.

ISBN: 9780170418409